CHASE

How to Connect with the Other Side to Find the Clarity and Confidence to Be Yourself

Elizabeth Kendig
& Monica Lawson

A POST HILL PRESS BOOK

Chase You:
How to Connect with the Other Side to Find the Clarity and Confidence to Be Yourself

ISBN: 978-1-63758-366-1
ISBN (eBook): 978-1-63758-367-8

Cover design by Cody Corcoran
Interior design and composition by Greg Johnson, Textbook Perfect

Post Hill Press
New York • Nashville
posthillpress.com

Published in the United States of America
1 2 3 4 5 6 7 8 9 10

For our husbands, Ty and Bill,
for believing,
AJ and Emily
for being the greatest teachers,
and for Hal.

Contents

PROLOGUE

I am sitting at a picnic table, typing on the laptop in front of me, piles of papers everywhere. The sun is shining. Mountains stretch before me. Am I on a ranch?

The wind is whipping up the papers. I reach out to stop them from flying away. I'm wearing an oversized cardigan straight out of the Big Lebowski.

Monica is walking toward me carrying a platter of BBQ ribs. She's beaming. I look back at my laptop. I'm writing a book for her.

Now we're both standing in a control room full of switchboards. A guy swivels around in his chair and plugs something into the wall. The entire room lights up, twinkling from floor to ceiling like a giant Lite Brite.

"This is what your book is going to do," he says. "Turn on people's lights everywhere."

I wake up. It's morning. My husband is in bed next to me, texting with a friend who's having us over for dinner that night.

"What is he making?" I ask.

Ribs.

CHAPTER 1

From Monica

"Get down . . . and pray."

These were the first words I heard them say. Then came a deep feeling that something really bad was about to happen. I crouched down on my seat, covered my eyes, started praying the Lord's prayer, and fainted.

It was December 20, 1978. I was nine years old. We were on our way to my grandparents' house, and a seemingly random chain of events had led me to be sitting in the front passenger seat. I am so grateful that I fainted because little did I know we would be in a horrific car accident that would catapult me through the front windshield—and onto my life path.

After we collided with the other car, I witnessed a series of beautifully divine interventions. Though unconscious, I could still hear someone asking, "Is she dead?"

I came to but couldn't see because there was so much blood on my face. I wanted to let them know I was alive, but before I could, I fainted again.

We were out in the middle of nowhere when a truck full of passengers stopped and my frantic mother decided to hand me over so they could take me to the hospital. Back then, no one had cell phones. My poor mother didn't know when or how an ambulance would get to us. She had blind faith and decided to entrust me with these kind strangers. I drifted in and out of consciousness during that ride but do not remember entering the hospital.

I would later learn that other cars had driven by the car accident and didn't stop. Only a white El Camino car with a male and female, both white-haired, wearing all white, would stop. They had a CB radio and called an ambulance for the rest of my family, who were also hurt. I now know that they, along with the passengers in the truck, were divinely sent by the Other Side to help us. I also believe that, based on their appearance, the couple were angels. They disappeared before my family could thank them.

I continued to come in and out of consciousness because of the pain. I had lost some of the skin around my forehead and eyebrow area from the impact. I also had huge amounts of glass all over my right eye. I remember wanting to "wake up" so the medical team would know I was alive but the pain from the glass being pulled out was so excruciating that I would faint again.

At this point, I kept hearing, "Try to relax, you are going to be okay." I knew it wasn't from the emergency room staff because I could clearly hear them too. This voice was coming from somewhere or someone else. I still didn't know who I was hearing, but it calmed me down. The energy behind the words was loving, reassuring, and peaceful.

I finally woke up and could tell that the doctors were still working on me. I looked to my left and saw that my baby sister, whose second birthday was that day, was lying on the table next to me. She was in shock, eyes wide open, and her face was bloodied and appeared to be covered in burn marks. The doctors and nurses were trying to get her to respond, but she just lay there completely still and unresponsive.

I reached out with my left hand to touch her because I thought she had died, only to faint again. This time, I felt and saw myself floating up and out of my body. I could still hear everyone working on us. Next thing I knew, I was watching them above from a corner in the room. I then felt a bright white light all around me, and I could hear talking.

I was still focused on what was going on in the emergency room but knew and could feel someone was behind me. As they came closer, I felt an immense amount of love. Words cannot do it justice. It was pure, unconditional love and happiness, the most peaceful thing I have ever experienced. The feeling shocked me into paying attention to it. I remember basking in this love because I had never felt anything like it before.

Then, I could sense beings all around me.

I instinctively and unequivocally knew that these beings were love who cared for me immensely and wanted to help me. Next, I felt a strong, immeasurably loving presence. It was different from the others. The massive energy is still indescribable. I knew it was God. He continued to let me bask in the light, look at and feel the beings around me, then asked me, "Do you want to stay?"

I immediately felt like jumping up and down and saying *YES!* I wanted to stay in the white light. Even when I looked down at the emergency room and my sister below, I couldn't talk myself into returning. You see, our life had been hard up to that point. Staying in this beautiful, immense love felt so much better.

I said, "Yes, I do want to stay."

That's when I heard God respond, "Well, you have something important to do there, and you have to go back, dear child."

I knew it was true. I knew I was here on earth to do something important, even if I wasn't sure what it was yet. For a split second, I wondered why I was even given the option to stay. Looking back on it now, I know that I was meant to experience heaven, loving spiritual beings, and God so that I could teach others about the Other Side and want to go back to it one day.

I decided to float in the overwhelming love energy one more time before I headed back. The spiritual beings walked me down and placed me back in my body. They sweetly waved goodbye, and I passed out again.

Ever since that day, I can hear, see, feel, and know the Other Side. I have decided to dedicate my life to helping others through this experience. I want humanity to know that there is a higher being and that the Other Side exists. That there is a beautiful place we all go to after our time here on earth. I want everyone to know that they are sent here for a very important reason...a mission. We all have important work to do. More importantly, everyone can hear, see, feel, and know the Other Side—including you.

You can communicate with your spiritual team, who can guide you to a joyous life here on earth if you allow and work with them. You are never alone because the Other Side is always with us. They are with us from the minute we arrive here to the minute we transition back over.

I have dedicated my life to working as a spiritual advisor with a focus on mission, spiritual teams, and teaching people how to cocreate life with the Other Side. During readings, I call in my spiritual team and the client's spiritual team. These teams consist of assigned guardian angels, spirit guides, Ascended Masters, arch angels, and our higher being. They provide the guidance that one needs to keep moving forward, to chase you. It is one of my greatest joys, and I am honored to call this part of my mission work.

My clients include eleven- to ninety-year-olds. They are tech execs and non-profit employees, doctors and lawyers, students and stay-at-home moms, Hollywood actors and producers, Grammy-winning singer-songwriters and spiritual teachers, volunteers and retirees. And all of them come to me with ultimately the same question: *Who am I and why am I here?* Many are searching for higher meaning in their lives, how they can authentically serve humanity and achieve more fulfillment and happiness. Even the clients who "have it all" are still searching. They know there has to be more to life.

It is in learning to work with the Other Side that their lives become filled with the joy and peace they're seeking. What they have known all along about why they are here is validated and unfolds as they embark on a spiritual path. I can literally see people's energy expand when they fully step into their soul's mission.

Every single person is extremely important to all of humanity and to this planet. You, too, are here on an important mission that you alone can complete. We all are here to love one another and work together for the betterment of this earth. That is the only way to evolve as a planet and species. Finally, I know from my work and witnessing the Other Side in action that you are unconditionally loved and guided beyond belief.

We wrote this book for you. For you to know that you truly matter and have an amazing role to play in the betterment of all. You came here with the ability to connect with the Other Side and experience the peace and love of knowing them. I can't wait to introduce you.

CHAPTER 2

From Elizabeth

Monica came into my life as most healers do: at the exact moment I needed her. I was in transition, newly divorced, weighing my next career move, and on a spiritual journey. When the student is ready, the teacher appears.

We were introduced by an acquaintance who had experienced Monica's gifts during her own crossroads. I can still remember sitting on a beach in North Carolina when she texted me Monica's contact info and implored me to book a session with her. Little did I know it was a divinely guided moment, the start of an unwavering friendship and shared mission.

At the time, all I knew was that Monica was a spiritual mentor, powerfully guided by the Other Side. Over the next seven years, through countless phone sessions and voice-memo lessons laced with her sweet Texas drawl, I learned to work with the Other Side on my own.

After the rib dream, we knew it was time. I was living proof that the lessons worked and the dream was the sign we needed to share those lessons with the world. That day, the student became the teacher and we became co-authors.

While Monica and I were writing this book, people would inevitably ask me what it was about. It took me a while to own the elevator pitch, partly because I was sheepish about telling strangers about the Other Side and their reaction (*You mean, like, angels?*) and partly because I was still trying to make sense of it myself. How did I get here and what business did I have writing about something that I still at times question?

I know that it's natural for authors to experience imposter syndrome. But writing this book has not only required faith in myself to adequately deliver a sacred message that many may resist or even reject, but it has also tested my faith in the very subject matter. If the Other Side exists, if they truly want what's best for me (and you), then why has this process been so hard?

During the six months that Monica and I worked on this book, I experienced bouts of sadness, anger, grief, and tests to my marriage. I had spent several years trying to build a healing business that, while successful in supporting people who sought holistic guidance, had drained my family emotionally and financially. We had invested everything back into the business and forgone having children or buying a house so that I could continue on my mission. Live my dream! Follow my purpose. And it had yet to pay off in any tangible way. This is not what I signed up for.

Writing this book would only prolong the sacrifices our family was making—and there was no guarantee anyone would read it, let alone buy it. Sure, I had a roof over my head and food on the table and healthcare benefits, but it's important to note that I wrote this book under some duress. To glamorize it or anything on the following pages would do you, the reader, a disservice.

This book was not the answer to my prayers. It was magical and exciting and creatively satisfying at times, yes, but it also very much felt like a test from the Other Side. How committed was I to using my gifts and story for good? How much trust was I willing to put in the Universe that *this* time my hard work and sacrifices would pay off?

The irony is not lost on me. When the student becomes the teacher, lessons must be relearned. Mine has been realizing that we can't know the outcome, even when we work with the Other Side, and that is by design. They are not the solution to all of our problems or a lottery ticket. Walking the spiritual path is only the beginning of the journey. What follows is like peeling back the layers of a never-ending onion—and it's not always an awesome blossom. The more you chase you, and a life of authenticity, the more courage will be required of you.

Writing this now, I still don't know how this book will be received. I saved writing this introduction for the final hours in the hopes that I would be able to tie it all up with bow and give you a happy ending. Alas, the only gift that I can offer is this: It's in the trying that we find ourselves. It's in the believing that you are enough and that you deserve to be happy, *come what may*, that the treasure lies. You can follow all of the wisdom of this book and enlist the Other Side, but the buck ultimately stops with you. The lessons in the book aren't as much a means to an end as a means to the beginning of what we believe will bring you a greater sense of peace, freedom, and purpose.

I know this because despite not having it all figured out in the decade since I began working with the Other Side, my life has changed dramatically for the better. In fact, I barely remember my life before I knew the Other Side because I wasn't really alive until I met them.

I had been low-key and, on a few occasions, clinically depressed for as long as I can remember.

One of my therapists called me the "walking wounded." Like a functioning alcoholic, I was a highly functioning depressed person. No one would've guessed because on the outside my life checked all the boxes: a loving family, plenty of friends, good grades, the best schools, and later, a successful career.

Even as a five-year-old who had everything she needed, I was sad. I often thought that God or whoever had made a mistake. I did not belong on Earth. It was so hard and unnatural for me. I didn't want to die, per se, but could I please be returned to sender?

Growing up, I watched other kids having fun, looking so carefree, and I just couldn't connect. I wasn't cute enough, funny enough, athletic enough, smart enough. My friends and younger brother seemed to take life in stride, so content and easygoing, whereas I was too emotional. Too sensitive. Too...extra. No matter what I did, how good my grades were, or how many girls came to my slumber parties, I was always on the outside looking in. More than anything, I felt profoundly alone. It's easy now to look back and see that girl with love and appreciation. She was bright, kind, curious, and open-hearted. She still is.

As an adult, my depression got real. For most of my life, I had combatted my pain and otherness with perfectionism and over-achieving. And it had worked—for a while. I had a six-figure beauty business and a BMW in the driveaway. I had finally found my people, whose deep and abiding friendship still sustains me. But there was no more hiding from an unhappy marriage, an autoimmune disease that resisted every traditional form of treatment, and a heightened sense that something was missing.

I would need to dig deeper if I ever wanted to thrive, not just survive.

I was fortunate enough to have a job as a magazine editor and blogger that gave me access to incredible healers. A colleague recommended an intuitive medium, Christine Schroeder, and after my first session, I was hooked. Finally, someone saw me. I wasn't a mistake! The Other Side made that clear in the reading, among other validations about my life up until that point.

Making contact with the spiritual world was the beginning of what I can best describe as a self-help bender, immersing myself in every spiritual and healing experience that I could get my hands on. I had my palms read, tarot cards pulled, chakras realigned, and akashic records opened. I saged my house, slept in a silk cocoon, and revisited past lives. (Maybe we met when I was a cowgirl in 15th-century Spain?) I tried sound bath therapy, equine therapy, and hypnotherapy too.

They all had one thing in common: with them, I felt connected to a higher power. A force beyond myself or anything physical. It wasn't religion or even God. There was a whole world beyond, and they got me. Saw me. And made it very clear there wasn't anything wrong with me. These spirit guides provided the love and support that until then I wasn't able to give myself.

Slowly, I started to feel . . . happy. My psoriasis cleared up. I quietly and amicably divorced. My relationship with my parents became a source of comfort and grounding instead of outworn teenage angst. And my relationship with myself was now rooted in acceptance and, on good days, actual love. I had become my own best friend, along with the Other Side. It was the first time in my life that I didn't feel alone.

And then I met Monica.

She taught me how to engage with my "Team" in a meaningful and methodical way that made sense to me. I didn't need special powers to access their guidance or assistance; they were available to me simply because I existed. From there, my life unfolded at a rapid pace and with greater purpose, joy, and flow.

Working with the Other Side led to all kinds of magical experiences and transformations. I could tell you that it fixed everything, but that jig is already up. I could, and will in future chapters, tell you that I met the love of my life and embarked on a new career that is even more aligned with my soul than the previous one. I moved across the country twice to cities I had only dreamed of living in. I fortified relationships with my friends and family in ways that bring me to tears.

But more than anything, I wake up every day with more peace than I have ever known. I am here for a reason, on purpose, and no longer have to go it alone. Knowing that the Other Side is standing by to guide and support me gives me the strength to move through life with a sense of purpose and freedom I didn't know was possible. With their help, there is nothing I can't do, be, or have if it is in my highest good. The same is true for you.

That is why we wrote this book and where we begin.

CHAPTER 3

Introduction: Why This Book

As a collective, we are tired of the chase. We are lonely, burnt out, and discontent despite doing and chasing all of the things we were told would make us happy.

We are also more anxious and depressed than ever before, with two in five adults reporting symptoms of anxiety or depression[1] and the suicide rate in the U.S. up 35 percent since 1999.[2]

Between a global pandemic, economic instability, a profound political divide, and a climate crisis, nothing we are chasing is a sure thing anymore. It never really was. And

---

1 Anjel Vahratian et al. "Symptoms of Anxiety or Depressive Disorder and Use of Mental Health Care Among Adults During the COVID-19 Pandemic," *Morbidity and Mortality Weekly Report* 70, no. 13 (2021): 490–494, DOI: http://dx.doi.org/10.15585/mmwr.mm7013e2external icon.

2 Holly Hedegaard, M.D., Sally C. Curtin, M.A., and Margaret Warner, Ph.D. "Suicide Mortality in the United States, 1999-2019," NCHS Data Brief, no. 398 (2021), DOI: https://dx.doi.org/10.15620/cdc:101761.

we are not the same people we were in The Before. We are waking up and wondering: *Is this all there is?!*

This book is about a different way of living and being. It's about chasing what will actually create more purpose and peace to your life: YOU.

We're here to remind you that YOU matter. YOU are already enough.

You came here to reach your full potential and to manifest your soul's destiny. Standing by to assist you is the Other Side. This Team of spiritual beings, which every human was assigned at birth, is here to help you know your authentic self and navigate life lessons so that you can live your mission. If you can suspend disbelief long enough to experience their support and remember who you came here to be, your life will begin to flow.

When you start chasing you, the rest will follow.

We know this because we've both implemented the practices in this book and our lives have transformed dramatically as a result. Monica has already taught hundreds of clients to do the same. Many of their stories appear on these pages.

This book is a how-to guide for working with the Other Side to create more peace, purpose, and joy in your life. If you've already got those in spades, then the practices on these pages can empower you to consciously cocreate even more. We trust that this book will find its way to the people who need it, so if you're reading this, there's a reason and it is perfect.

Although we wrote this book to help you enrich your experience here on earth, we hesitate to call it a "self-help" book because that implies that there is something wrong with you. That you need fixing. The constant quest for self-improvement can take you further away from becoming more, well, you.

We aren't here to tell you who that is or what to be. Our views and preferences—from religion to politics to how much hot sauce I put on everything—are not important or relevant to your story. If we sprinkle them in, it's to provide context and reinforce that we are having a human experience complete with very human struggles, just like you.

Only you can choose who to be or what you want out of life. We'll be teaching you how to access the guidance of the Other Side on those decisions and desires both big and small. It's yours if you want it, and it's available to everyone who asks.

What This Book Is Not

This is not a get-rich-quick book, a medical cure, a manifestation manual, or a psychic primer—though you'll definitely develop your intuition along the way.

We will not suggest that you quit your job, leave your marriage, or move to Bali—though you may decide to do one or all of the above. That's between you and the Other Side. And, because we all have free will, entirely up to you.

We are not here to wave a magic wand and or make all of your dreams come true. We don't have any special powers, only a responsibility to teach you what we've learned so that you can implement the lessons for yourself.

What we can promise is that whatever you want out of life, you don't have to go it alone. The Other Side wants to cocreate with you, support and guide you.

But you won't have to take our word for it. In fact, you shouldn't. Implementing the lessons in this book is how you'll develop trust that the Other Side is real, that your spirit guides want only the best for you, and that working with them is a powerful path to freedom. Our job isn't to convince you but to show you how.

How To Use This Book

Learning to work with the Other Side isn't hard, and you can't mess it up, but there is a method to our madness. The book outlines the steps that Monica has learned from working with her guides and taught to hundreds of clients of all ages and backgrounds. It's intentionally designed to be easy because we want everyone to be able to use it.

Each chapter is designed to build on the next, giving you the tools to grow your connection with the Other Side. It's through practice that you'll learn to spot the signs and gain trust in yourself and your spirit guides. Jumping around is fun—we get the urge—but you will have a much more fulfilling and fruitful experience if you read this book chronologically.

That said, there is no rush. Stick with a chapter for as long as you need. Practice the lessons as much as you want! Your guides live for this stuff. If something isn't resonating, put the book down and come back to it. Your guides aren't going anywhere.

The experiences, steps, and true stories we'll share throughout this book are designed to assist you in developing your own dialogue with the Other Side. Everyone's will be different.

Once you've followed our steps to meeting them and have the hang of working with them, you can revisit any chapter or passage as needed for guidance, validation, and inspiration.

Our wish for you is to fully embrace who YOU came here to be. This book is a framework for writing your own story, with a big assist from the Other Side. We're honored to be the messengers.

CHAPTER 4

Meet Your Team: An Introduction to the Other Side

You and every single human on earth are here on a mission. You signed up for it before you were born. You are here to help heal, teach, and serve a community. You are also here for soul growth lessons. In choosing to come here, you were given a spiritual team on the Other Side to assist you on your mission. We call them the Team.

Your Team is here to guide and protect you during your time here on earth. They know you, they see you, and they believe in you unconditionally. They want nothing but the best for you. At this very moment, your Team is standing by to help you fulfill your mission.

The Team exists regardless of your religious or spiritual beliefs. They will be with you from the moment you are born to the moment you cross over, no matter what you do, who you worship, or how you spend your life. Your Team is your Team; they will never leave your side.

Your Team is here to assist you with your soul growth, those life lessons that seem to follow us around until we finally learn them. You know the ones: insecurities, fear, anger, shame...the stories we tell ourselves and patterns we repeat no matter what job we take, how much money we make, or new relationships we start. Your Team is here to assist with identifying and healing these wounds. Why? Because the sooner you do, the more joyful and in flow life becomes.

Your Team also wants you to know that you're never alone. So many of us go through life thinking that we are on our own. That the only person looking out for us is ourselves. That aloneness can show up as not feeling like you fit in, or that the Universe/God made a mistake sending you here, when in fact you are here on purpose. Once you feel their presence and experience their support you'll never feel alone again.

You may already intuitively sense that there's a Team. You may have already felt or experienced them but don't have the words or tangible proof to confirm their existence. Monica is our here-on-earth messenger. She can see our Teams along with her own team.

Who's On Your Team

Guardian Angels

We each have two guardian angels who are with us from birth and never leave our side. They are the same angels from the minute you get here until you transition back over. You can think of them with or without wings—they still aren't going anywhere!

Your angels' job is to protect and keep you out of danger. They talk to you through your gut. Those hunches, instincts, inexplicably bad vibes you get about a situation or person—that's your angels. They'll keep you from going down a dark alley, talking to an unstable stranger, or anything that could disturb your peace or safety. For example: when you feel or maybe even hear a voice in your head say *slow down* while driving, it could be to avoid an accident or a speeding ticket. You could also be packing for a trip and feel or hear to take a particular thing. You might think it's silly to take a raincoat to the desert, but for some reason, you end up needing it. Guardian angels can see up ahead for us. They know what we will be encountering and will work their magic to assist us or avoid anything that will disturb our peace. If you take anything away from this chapter, let it be to never dismiss and always trust your gut feelings, even when they don't make sense.

Spirit Guides

Spirit guides have walked the earth. They come and go depending on what you need. Since they have had human experiences here on earth, they are here to help you with anything physical. That could be which apartment to rent, where to go to school, giving you all green lights when you're running late, or even a front row-parking spot. You can ask for their assistance when you are tackling a home project, preparing for an interview or presentation you're giving, or trying to decide where to go on vacation.

Your spirit guides will send you messages through dreams, repetitive messages, synchronicities/coincidences, musical messages, helpful people, and numbers. They also love to send you feathers, coins, and animals as confirmation and messages.

Ascended Masters

Ascended Masters are here to help you master your unique way of living and communicate through their teachings. They will change throughout your life as you grow and evolve. Examples of Ascended Masters include Buddha, Jesus, Mother Earth, and the spiritual teachers of your chosen faith. Whoever's philosophies or teachings resonate with you is most likely nearby, waiting to connect and work with you. If you're drawn to a specific book or documentary or can't get enough of a certain subject or practice, it's often a clue of what to study and embrace. If you get signs repeatedly (i.e., someone invites you on a meditation retreat after you tell your wife for the fifteenth time that you really want to start meditating), dig deep and study. It's part of your life path, and the Ascended Masters will be walking alongside you.

Archangels

Archangels come and go to help us through major life transitions such as birth, death, healing, a new job, marriage, divorce, etc. Each has a particular function/specialty area, depending on what you need help with or who is with you.

You may already be familiar with some, such as Archangel Michael, but did you know that you can call on him to release fear and doubt and boost your courage and self-esteem when making a life change? Busy guy.

You can have more than one archangel with you at all times. The archangel who is here to help you with your mission never leaves your side. The others come and go depending on life's transitions. They communicate with you via feelings, colors, and sometimes quick specs of lights. We encourage you to seek out your archangels when you are struggling in a particular area of life. They can send physical signs, like the right book at the right time, as well as emotional and spiritual support like a therapist or Reiki healer when you need one most. They love nothing more than to help you.

Your Higher Power

There is a higher power who loves and assists you unconditionally. You can call them whatever feels true for you: God, Allah, Spirit, Universe, Source, etc. They want to help keep you balanced so you can continue on your path and purpose. For example, when we go through something difficult, they will assist us to turn it into something of service, if we so choose.

This higher power sent us here to assist one another in our development and growth. They gave each one of us a mission that serves humanity. Their hope and plan for us is to grow, love one another, and assist in the evolution of humanity. This evolution will bring us all closer together, in which every single human, state, and country assists one another and works as a collective for the betterment of humanity and the planet.

Your higher power ensured that every single one of us came to earth with gifts to share with the world. We are each a piece of a single, larger puzzle. The quicker we learn this and start living as a collective instead of in separation, the quicker humanity and this planet will shift into a more peaceful alignment. We are not here to be separate. We are here to live as one.

Our higher power communicates with us through divine timing, open and closed doors, miracles, peace, love, and support.

Loved Ones and Ancestors

When our loved ones cross over, they remain with us in spirit. You can communicate with them any time, and they will always send you signs that they are with you. They can come to you in your dreams, send animals and nature signs, work through electricity and even your iPhone, and, if you're open and listening, can even be heard speaking to us.

They are always with you, loving you unconditionally, supporting your endeavors and letting you know that the other side is very real. If you are open to it, you can experience the signs they send. For example, if you are thinking about a transitioned loved one, the lights could flicker, or a song that you or they loved will come on the radio. What seems like a crazy coincidence is actually them, and the more you acknowledge the messages and signs your loved ones send, the more they will engage with you. Children are really open at a young age and can definitely see them. So if your child says something about Grandpa being in the room, believe them and pay attention!

Your Team on Earth

While you are given a spiritual team, you are also sent supporting team members on Earth who assist you in physical ways. They, too, play an important role on your journey.

We are assigned human beings to deliver us messages from the Other Side, help us transition from one life phase to another, and for our growth and healing. These humans can be family, friends, partners, strangers, coworkers, and even those who are widely dehumanized by society.

Never turn your eyes, ears or heart away from someone who challenges you or your comfort zone because they could be delivering a message or here to teach you a critical lesson. Even your children are little messengers, so pay attention to them, even (and especially) when they push your buttons.

Our pets are also sent to us. They can provide unconditional love, emotional and health support, and teach us how to live and be. Our pets are sent to us to enhance our lives, and we in turn enhance theirs. They are one of the most beautiful teachers we can be gifted.

We all play a role in each other's evolution as well as the planet's. Anyone and anything can be used as a messenger, so always pay attention and treat others with kindness and respect; you just never know who the Other Side put in your path to help you!

EXERCISE: Confirming that Your Team Exists

At this point in the book, we have zero delusions that you believe a word we are saying. *A Team? Angels? Next, are you going to tell me that there are fairies and warlocks?* Wait. Don't answer that.

We would never want or expect you to take our word for it. Monica was a total cynic when she started this process. She tested her Team for *months* and threw lots of side eye before trusting that they existed. For me, this exercise was an instant gateway drug, which is one reason our relationship works.

Your skepticism will serve you well. It's an essential part of this process. Until you confirm and believe that your Team is real, you won't trust their signs and messages. We still like to test our Team because the confirmation process is a magical one and always reaffirms our faith.

You can repeat this exercise as many times as you want or need to until you feel confident–or at least cautiously optimistic—that your Team exists. You can also take a break and come back to it when you're ready. Your Team won't tire of this exercise or give up on you. In other words: this offer does not expire.

Dear Team: if you do exist, send me a (object) within a week.

An object is anything tangible, like a feather, coin, red balloon, animal, candy, etc. Don't overthink it! Choose an object you love or the first one that pops in your head.

Give it a week, no longer, to receive the item. If for some reason you don't receive it, ask for something different. It could be that you missed it and/or it was too hard for them to arrange for its delivery. (But we applaud your creativity!) They do have to move mountains to get our objects to us, so start simple. There will be plenty of time to test them later!

Remember to be completely open to the process. You could receive a physical feather, coin, animal, or you could see a picture of one on a wall, in print, online, or someone could even point the object out to you without knowing the significance. Your Team will deliver the thing you requested in the quickest and easiest manner possible.

Once you've connected with your Team and confirmed their existence, you're ready to actively cocreate with them. It's never too soon or too late to start. (Just ask Monica's ninety-year-old clients!) Whenever you decide to experience the magic of your Team, and accept the help they are standing by to provide you, the more you'll want to work with them. Let's get started!

Elizabeth

The first time I tested this theory, I thought it would be cute to give my Team an impossible challenge: show me three butterflies in three days. In February. In Minnesota, where I was living at the time. Good luck!

Day one: I was at the gym, reading the *New York Times* on the elliptical (I never said this was a story about effective workouts). The first paragraph of the first article mentioned butterflies.

Day two: A friend called to tell me about her amazing acupuncture appointment, including that the office walls were painted with butterflies.

Day three: It was evening and I was getting discouraged. Where could a third butterfly sign possibly come from—a snowstorm? I turned on *Top Chef Mexico*. For one of their challenges, the chefs were taking a field trip...to a butterfly sanctuary. I stared at the screen. There were butterflies everywhere.

Kate

After a reading with Monica, Kate wanted her Team to prove to her that they, indeed, exist.

As she got in her car and drove away from the reading, Kate asked to hear or see the words "dream team" three times within three days. She said, *If you really exist, I need to hear or see dream team.*

When Kate got home, she put her keys and purse down on the kitchen counter. In the next room, her husband was watching a basketball game, and she heard the announcer say "the dream team."

The next day, Kate went to work and a colleague said he wanted to put together a dream team of attorneys on a particular case.

On the third day, Kate picked up her kids along with one of their friends. All three were sitting in the back seat talking about sports, and the friend said something about several players coming together to make a dream team.

After that, Kate had no doubt that her guides existed and started working with them. To this day, she still calls them her Dream Team.

Emily

When she was twelve years old, Emily wanted to test out if her Team really existed. She was in middle school. She asked her Team to send her a feather in a surprising or strange way.

That Friday night while in the swimming pool with friends, a feather fell from the sky into her hands.

She was in shock, and like any curious middle schooler, wanted to test them again.

That same night, Emily asked to be given a quarter in an unexpected way. The next morning, she had to be at school very early to get ready to travel to the art competition at another school. She was the first to arrive, so she waited outside until her teacher arrived to unlock the door. When they walked into the classroom, Emily went to her desk and found—you guessed it—a quarter sitting squarely on her desk.

Now, nineteen and in college where she's still studying art, Emily often asks for signs from her beloved grandmother, Ma, who passed away three years ago. They always arrive in beautiful ways.

One Christmas Eve, she got a text in the middle of the night from a new friend who didn't know anything about her grandmother. All it said was: MA. The next morning her friend followed up with a text saying *oops, not sure how that happened! I didn't even send that.*

Recently, when Emily got to class, her professor put up a slide titled "The Concept of Ma."

Our loved ones are always with us; you simply need to ask!

CHAPTER 5

How to Work with the Other Side: Three Signs in Three Days

Now that you've met your Team and given them permission to assist you, it's time to start working with them. This is the fun part! Where you'll get to see your guides in action and just how deep their support for you runs. It's also where you'll learn something even more important: how to trust yourself.

Your Team is always ready and excited to work with you. They are a beautiful lifeline for you available at all times. You are never alone. They are always with you and can't wait to assist you with anything and everything. They want more than anything to work with you. It's not only their wish, but their job. Can you imagine someone sitting around just waiting for you to ask them for help and having all the answers!? That's your Team.

If it sounds like snake oil or too good to be true, you're in the right place. There's nothing we can tell you or try to convince you of that will be more compelling than experiencing the Team for yourself. Once you establish a connection and the signs and synchronicities begin to appear everywhere, the magic will be undeniable, and your life will never be the same.

The Team is also here to help you remember your truth and trust yourself. We are all looking for answers or someone to tell us what to do. *Should I take the job? Quit my job? Buy the house? Move across the country? Go on another date with that guy who cracked a weird cat joke and listens to country music?* (Nothing against cats or country!)

We're afraid to mess up, to get it wrong. To get it "right," we obsess. We analyze. Phone a friend. Poll our Facebook followers. Ask our therapist. Consume self-help books (ahem). Heart inspirational Instagram quotes. Phone another friend. Some of us become so paralyzed with fear that we never actually make a decision. We stay exactly where we are, swaddled in our soft pants. No change means nothing can go wrong.

This is completely natural and understandable. From an early age, we learn to question ourselves and stop trusting our inner guidance system because everyone around us has an opinion. We are bombarded by them from the media, our parents, teachers, and strangers on the internet. Our own voice and innate optimism have been drowned out by louder voices and stripped away but away with external noise and louder voices, no matter how well meaning, and strong opinions.

Your Team can help you reclaim the childlike sense of wonder you were born with and to trust yourself again so that you can live with more flow and less fear, knowing that your choices are aligned with YOU. They want to empower you and validate your inner compass, not replace your personal agency. They want you to chase you.

Think of your Team as way-showers on your life path, pointing out the sights and experiences along the way that will make for the most beautiful and fulfilling trip. From finding a new dentist to discovering your mission, your Team is here to support you on the journey. They can open doors for you, connect you with people or partners you're meant to meet, and reveal career paths or creative outlets that will bring you a sense of purpose. No matter who you are or what you're going through, your Team is always a call away—for big decisions, life transitions, when you feel stuck, or when you simply need a good parking spot.

But first, you have to ask.

Monica

When I started doing this work, I kept having recurring dreams in which the Other Side told me that I was a shaman. At the time, I had no idea what that meant. I even fought the idea! But the dreams persisted.

When I told my mom about the dreams, her response shocked me. She thought that I might be a shaman too. She told me that she had been raised by her great aunt whom she called Mama Nana. Mama Nana, a Native American, had shamanic powers and would use them to help people in the area where she lived in Mexico.

After hearing this story, I said to my Team: *Okay, if I am truly a shaman and need to study shamanism to enhance my skills, I need to hear the word Shaman three times within three days.*

The signs started pouring in.

The next day, at an appointment that I had scheduled weeks prior, a local intuitive reader told me that I am a shaman. I was floored.

Later that day, I was watching television and a shaman appeared on the show.

The following day, I was having a reiki session when the reiki master invited me to a shaman drum circle.

The following week, a client called me her "chic-y shaman." At this point, I could hardly argue!

And the signs kept coming.

That week, I scheduled a phone session with an Akashic reader recommended by a local spiritual shop. I had no idea what an Akashic reader was at that time and she, too, told me that I was a shaman.

That same week, another client called me a shaman.

My daughter came home and told me she was reading a book at school about a shaman.

See where this is going?

After I finally embraced their call to action (or my mission?), the Team started sending me the teachers, classes, books, and tools to support my shamanic studies.

That was a decade ago, and I'm so glad I trusted the signs.

Three Signs in Three Days

Monica teaches a simple, three-step process for communicating with your Team: acknowledge, ask, and affirm. We're sharing this process to give you structure and confidence, knowing that in time, you may develop your own language with the Other Side. They may even be communicating with you already without you realizing it, and this exercise will help illuminate their messages!

1. Acknowledge

The first step is to acknowledge your Team and grant them permission to help you. They cannot intervene on your behalf unless you give them permission. Even if you don't believe they exist yet, acknowledge your guides, thank them for being with you, and grant them permission to help you. The minute you do, the synchronicity starts, and we start flowing through life.

Say the following out loud or silently:

> *I'm calling in my guardian angels, my spirit guides, my Ascended Masters, archangels, and higher being. I grant you permission to help me in any shape or form. Thank you for helping me.*

Ideally, do this every time you work with your Team. Think of it as an opening prayer or meeting kick-off. You're now ready to start working with your Team.

2. Ask

Secondly, you're going to ask your Team to send you the same sign three times within three days. This is how you'll receive directional guidance.

Why three signs and why three days? We could give you a bunch of woo-y reasons about the number three being sacred or Monica seeing 333 spelled out with seashells in the sand, but to be honest, it's because we are naturally cynical human beings like everyone else, and one sign is not enough, nor is one day always long enough for the Team to get its act together. It's also much harder to argue with three signs.

If you have a question about yourself or your life, your Team most likely has the answer. There's not much that's off limits when it comes to asking for a sign—as long as it comes from an authentic place and it's about or for you.

No question is too silly or too serious for your Team. You could ask about what toothpaste to buy (*have you seen the toothpaste aisle lately?*), but more likely, you're going to engage your Team when you need help or have a more pressing question.

We recommend starting with a simple, straightforward question. *Where should I go on vacation?* is going to yield a much clearer response when you're new to working with signs than, say, asking about your life purpose.

If you find yourself overthinking the question, simply *ask for your next step*. Your Team will respond with what you need to do next to realign with yourself.

Here's your script:

Dear Team/Spirit Guides/Universe: Please send me the same sign three times within three days about ________. Thank you!

IMPORTANT: Be sure to ask an open-ended question, not a leading or yes/no question (i.e., *Should I apply to be on The Bachelor?*). You probably know the answer, but this is to avoid confirmation bias.

3. Affirm

Finally, give the Team permission to hit you over the head with the signs. Affirm that you want them to give you the clarity and circumstances to see the signs, so you don't miss them and you know they're from your Team.

Doing so will encourage your Team to make sure you turn your head to notice a billboard, park next to a car with a bumper sticker meant for you, or turn on the radio at the exact right time to hear a song with some significance.

Then you let go and wait to receive your signs!

AJ

AJ was trying to decide between two colleges. He asked his Team to show him which one to attend by sending three signs in three days.

The first night, AJ had a dream that he was being chased in the woods by a bear. The bear meant nothing to him at the time, but he took note and kept it in his back pocket in case the information made sense later.

The next day, he was hanging out with my extended family. When AJ's aunt went to leave, she said, "Omg I just remembered something. I had a dream that I was walking my dogs and a bear was chasing me. What do you think that means?"

Huh. Two bears.

On the third day, AJ's godson showed up at church wearing a bear costume.

Now it clicked: the bear was the mascot of one of his college picks.

To be safe, he asked for three more signs and received those as well. He started there that fall.

How Signs Show Up

Signs come in all kinds of formats and from all manner of sources. While a sign could literally be a street sign, more often they appear in less obvious ways. The fewer expectations you have for what your signs will look like or how they will appear, the better. Staying open will help ensure you don't miss them! Here are some common examples:

- Animals, birds, insects, pets
- Words, symbols, logos, numbers
- Books, magazines, product packaging
- Movies, TV, podcasts, apps, social media
- Music: on the radio, Spotify, playing in a store, bar, or restaurant, when you get in the car
- An actor or TV or radio host says or does something
- Family, friends, coworkers say or do something
- Strangers say or do something: in a store, coffee shop, on the street, Uber driver
- An email, text, or social media message or comment you receive
- Physical signs: banners, posters, billboards, license plates, bumper stickers, menus
- While dreaming or meditating

How the Team Works

You will see or hear the same sign or clue three times within three days. That doesn't mean that every sign will appear to you in the same way, in the same format or at the same time each day. Your guides work in their own way and on their own schedule and often have a sense of humor.

You may get two signs the first day and nothing again until the third. Or all three on the same day. Any combination or variation counts. If you only get two after three days, it's safe to say you missed one somewhere and that's your sign. You can even ask again if you need to see it a third time to be utterly convinced. Whatever you do, don't go looking or searching for your signs. They will come to you when you least expect it—that is part of the magic!

Always, ALWAYS pay attention to recurring themes, like hearing the same song again and again or three different people suggesting a book or author to you. With practice, you'll learn to spot these themes even faster and find that your Team may rely on signs that it knows you'll easily recognize or identify with.

Elizabeth

My husband, Ty, and I moved to Brooklyn six weeks after we got married. We packed up our condo and our dog and drove across the country to the city I had always dreamt of living in and where we planned to spend the rest of our lives.

I was in talks with potential business partners there, and Ty was interviewing for jobs in an industry and market he had been working in for twenty years. We had even found the perfect apartment, sight unseen. Everything felt meant to be and a sure thing.

Almost a year later, my business deal had dissolved, Ty hadn't found a job, and we had drained our savings. The move we had pinned all of our hopes on and the life we had been so certain of was unraveling. Why was this happening? I couldn't help but think there was a reason, a plan yet to be revealed to us.

Then, a month before our lease was up, Ty was recruited for a job in San Francisco. It was a fantastic opportunity but so far away from our friends and family and the future we'd envisioned we almost didn't consider it.

When the job became a distinct possibility, we asked our Teams for signs. We didn't need them to make the decision for us, but we did need validation that it was the right decision and that it was happening for our highest good.

The next day, the first email in my inbox said "San Francisco" in the subject line. It had nothing to do with the move—just a random press release. Sign one.

That afternoon, Ty found himself walking down the streets of Brooklyn behind a guy wearing a California Republic t-shirt.

A few days later, he was in a bar and the San Francisco Giants were playing on the TV.

We had our three signs in rapid succession but were going to need more validation than that for a move this big.

I asked my father-in-law for guidance. He had passed away several years prior and often showed up as a bird when we needed him. Now I needed him to confirm that it was time to go West.

After making my request, single feathers started showing up on the streets of Brooklyn, in places where birds rarely fly and feathers don't belong.

As the days passed and it looked like a job offer was imminent, the feathers started coming faster.

One morning, I stepped out onto our back patio and it was covered in piles of feathers. Actual fistfuls. I hate to think about what happened to the bird, but there was no mistaking the message.

My husband took the job, and we've happily resided in the Bay Area for four years. Turns out, it's a place my father-in-law had always wanted to live but never got the chance to.

Tips for Working with Your Team

Monica gets a lot of questions about how to prepare to work with your Team. We cannot stress enough that you can't mess it up. You can ask while brushing your teeth, hugging a tree, taking a bath, holding a crystal, walking the dog. There are, however, a few simple practices that will get you in a more focused and grounded state of mind to connect with your guides.

Establish a Sacred Space

Establish a sacred space and time to connect with your Team. This lets them know that you are ready to work with them. Your sacred space can literally be anywhere that is a quiet space for you. It can be a corner in a room, outside in nature, your office, etc. People and things hold energy, so it's ideal if the space is clear of noise and clutter.

Find a space where your world slows down that's conducive to stillness and respite. Elizabeth is a big fan of talking to her Team in the bathtub for this reason. Make sure you grant yourself permission to slow down and be present. You will come to view these moments as sacred and your conversations with the Team a lifeline. It's like calling a meeting with your Team, and, no matter where you are or what time it is, they'll always show up.

Get Centered

Once you are in your sacred space, get centered. The more centered and free of distraction you are, the clearer your connection will be. Sit comfortably in your space, close your eyes, and put your hands on your belly or in a comfortable position. Take a few deep, cleansing breaths. Really concentrate on each breath as this will help you release any tension you might be holding.

Continue breathing until your body feels completely relaxed. You may even scan your body to see if you are holding any tightness. If you are, then breathe into the areas and release the tension. When you feel calmer and more centered, you'll be more open to receiving.

Get Clear

Lastly, get clarity on the area or question for which you'd like to receive guidance. Take some time to articulate what you would like to ask or know. It's best to work with one straightforward question at a time. If you haven't done so already, we strongly recommend that you go back to the previous chapter and start by asking them to confirm to you that they exist and are with you.

The more you work with your Team, the more easily you'll be able to identify the signs and trust your guides as well as your inner voice. Once you learn to flex this spiritual muscle, you'll be ready for your next assignment: discovering your mission.

CHAPTER 6

Other Ways to Work with the Other Side

Working with the Other Side, knowing you're not alone and can call on your Team for guidance, is like putting on an oxygen mask.

With time, practice, and trust, your interactions with your Team may evolve into an ongoing dialogue. You can continue using the three-signs-in-three-days exercise, or you can begin to cultivate your own spiritual conversation/language with your Team. Elizabeth likes to shout PLEASE SEND HELP from the bathtub.

As long as you've connected with your Team and given them permission to communicate with you, they'll respond in kind with signs and solutions. They may also connect with you through images or intuitive hints during meditation or prayer, in your dreams, or while journaling. Some people even get physical chills as validation of truths.

The more you get in the habit of paying attention, the more you'll pick up on the signs, and the process will become second nature. If you're unsure of the meaning or whether you can trust a message, ask for confirmation. Your Team will keep the clues coming.

Here are a few examples of how you can work with your Team to solve financial challenges, follow your dreams, and find love. As you'll see, there is nothing the Other Side won't assist you with when it's in your highest good.

Call them in. Ask them for your next step or what you need to move forward. Then let them do their job and expect miracles—though the miracle may not be what you expected.

Layla: Be Open to the Solution

Monica's client Layla was worried she wouldn't have enough money for a down payment for her new house. She had spent months worrying about it. Monica instructed her to relax and ask her Team to bring her a solution. Layla had no idea how her Team would possibly come through, but she made her request and patiently trusted.

A couple of months went by, and Layla landed a new consulting gig that would pay her the *exact* amount she needed for her down payment.

Bill: Follow the Breadcrumbs

Bill, a chiropractor, wanted to give back to the community in Marfa, Texas. Marfa had been a vacation destination for him for many years, and visiting brought him such great peace and solitude. He wanted to give back to the community that had given him so much joy. He was trying to decide how he was going to pay it forward when he noticed that healthcare was very limited in the small town. He wondered if there would be a way that he could serve the community that would benefit everyone involved and asked his Team to bring him a plan, including a place to work and easy logistics—the two things he needed to make it happen.

Back at his office, Bill was talking about Marfa to a patient. The massage therapist who worked for him at the time overheard the conversation and made a comment that her cousin, Suzi, lived in Marfa.

At the same time this conversation was happening, the receptionist walked into Bill's office with a message from a patient *who had just moved to Marfa.*

Bill called the patient back, and she explained to him that she had a friend who wanted to bring a chiropractor to Marfa. Suzi was opening a wellness community center with yoga, meditation, and massage, and had been asking the locals what else they wanted to see in her space. They said a chiropractor. Was Bill interested? Her friend's name, by the way, was Suzi. Yes, that Suzi.

Bill knew a sign (or three, as it were) when he saw one and said yes. He arranged a time to meet with Suzi in Marfa. The only questions would be finding affordable housing for his monthly trips there and setting up a payment system for the chiropractic services that would be easy for all parties involved.

Bill arrived in Marfa early, so he decided to grab a bite before the meeting. He walked into the restaurant and saw some friends he had made in Marfa. They explained that they had just bought the building across the street with four apartments on the top floor and that a wellness center was going to be downstairs. Guess who was running it?

Suzi.

When Bill shared that he was hoping to treat patients there, the friends offered to rent him one of their apartments. They wanted to support his mission and their town. At their first meeting, Suzi also suggested the payment system Bill had been hoping for.

He worked in Marfa every month for the next three years.

AJ: Listen to Your Inner Voice

Remember AJ who got the three bear signs about where to go to college? Once he decided to attend, he received scholarships, but the tuition to the private university still required a large out-of-pocket sum each month.

After asking his Team for money to help pay the tuition, AJ's parents received a hunch that they should visit the financial aid office in person to discuss his options instead of calling.

They drove to campus and arrived midday to find that AJ's financial aid officer was out to lunch. The front desk offered for them to meet with someone else. They went to his office, thanked him, and inquired if there were more financial aid options available for AJ that didn't involve taking out a loan.

The financial aid counselor looked up AJ's file and was surprised to discover that he had just been awarded a grant that morning that significantly offset his out-of-pocket tuition. In fact, there was a sticky note on his computer monitor with all the details. He awarded the grant to AJ on the spot.

Elizabeth: Pay Attention to Your Dreams

I had been working with Monica for only a few months when I told my Team I was ready for a relationship. I had been dating casually after a divorce but was looking for Big Love. A partner in crime to spend my life with. I didn't care if I was forty or eighty when I found him, I just knew he was out there. I asked my Team for help—and then let it go. I can't stress this enough. Holding on loosely and having faith that what is in your highest good will find its way to you when the time is right allows it to flow to you. Impatience, panic, a sense of something lacking—these are a recipe for pushing away what you want, not receiving it.

Not long after, I had a dream. Clearly, this is the way my Team likes to communicate with me. In the dream, I was standing in a bar. There weren't any ribs, but there was a man seated across the room. I couldn't see his face, but somehow I knew he was handsome. I couldn't hear his voice, but somehow I knew he was the funniest, kindest, most loving human I had ever met. Just being in that bar with him filled me with joy and a happiness that I didn't know was possible. What I could make out was what he was wearing: a button-down shirt under a zip-up sweater, topped with a sport coat (this was peak J.Crew prep).

An older woman came up behind me. I instantly knew she was one of my spirit guides. She put her hand on my shoulder and whispered, "Go over there and talk to him. That's your husband."

I shot up in bed and can still recall every detail vividly when I close my eyes. But mostly the feeling that the Other Side had just shown me my soulmate.

There still wasn't anything I could really do with this information except trust that he was coming. That the Team had received my request. I knew that the next steps would be revealed and went about my life.

Several months later, a friend texted me about a friend-of-a friend who had recently moved to town from NYC and was perfect for me. "The set-up of the century!" she said. Obviously, the first thing I did was Google him.

The next thing I did was fall off the couch.

In the search results was a LinkedIn headshot of the most adorable man wearing...a button-down shirt under a zip-up sweater, topped with a sport coat. It was the EXACT SAME outfit from my dream, right down to the window pane pattern of the shirt.

Seven years later, it's still hanging in our closet.

I could write another book about everything that happened in between—some of which you've already read in this book—but what you're really wondering is how long I waited to tell him about the dream.

Long enough to know that I had met my match and that he wouldn't be scared off by another one of my spiritual stories.

The Other Side can't make you fall in love. It can't make another person love you. But it can leave breadcrumbs to help you find each other. You get to decide whether to follow them.

CHAPTER 7

Loved Ones on the Other Side

Our loved ones that cross back over to the Other Side are still with us. They can communicate with us, are with us during special occasions, and they protect us. They, too, are part of our team.

There are different ways that departed loved ones communicate with us. They can appear in your nightly dreams. You can ask them for signs. Some people can also smell the person's favorite perfume, or if the loved one baked something special, you might still get a waft of their signature apple pie. If the loved one had a favorite song and it pops up on the radio, that's them saying hello.

Monica had a young client who had lost her mom at a very early age. She was upset that she was starting to forget her mom. Monica told her to ask that parent for a sign to let her know that they were with her. A couple of days later, she texted Monica a photo of dragonflies all around her. She had a special connection of dragonflies with this parent, who had sent her the swarm.

Sometimes our loved ones will make an appearance. Have you ever been in public and swear you've spotted a deceased loved one in the crowd? Or you're driving and a person walking down the street resembles your loved one? That's them. For a split second, they can appear to you.

Sometimes our loved ones send us signs without us asking them to.

Emily

When my grandmother, Ma, passed away, I was eighteen years old and a few weeks shy of my high school graduation—something she tried desperately to hold out for. I spent months asking for a morsel of attention from her once she passed but was only ever met with the absence of her presence. I think it took three to four months before I felt her spirit near again, and once I received one sign through my patient persistence, they continued most often without me even having to ask.

Ma was incredibly fond of the color yellow and butterflies, always reassuring me that I could find her warmth when butterflies were near. The first moment, or sign, that I experienced had me questioning everything I was skeptical of—for the better. Spending time outside was the easiest way for me to grieve her death, so I would frequent the natural springs of Austin, Texas on a weekly basis.

I remember going to St. Edward's Park, a park named after the university I would be attending in a few weeks, sitting and sulking where the sand met the waterline. I was in the angry phase of grief, wishing she would be there to help me move into my first college dorm, when a yellow butterfly the size of a softball appeared. Butterflies aren't creatures to linger, but this one allowed me to scoop it up and stayed in my hand for the rest of the thirty minutes I sat there.

As a professed skeptic, I hid my emotional excitement and thought if the butterfly meant something, if it was truly Ma, I would hear or see more.

And I did.

Fast-forward to my first day of undergrad. I'm in a rigorous sculpture class learning about a Japanese ceramic artist who creates vessels he calls *dangos*. As my eyes glossed over with boredom, I did a double take: on the screen was the word "MA" in bold Arial font. The artist, Jun Kaneko, speaks of Ma as the Japanese concept for lack of space, emptiness, absence. Fitting—but still not enough to convince me.

It took a third sign, a text message from a bot, to really cement that Ma could still communicate with me from the Other Side. It was Christmas morning, our first without Ma in her matching pajama set crying over something she's eternally grateful for. The house was solemn, blanketed in an unavoidable thick silence, abruptly cut by a text notification from my phone. A random amalgamation of numbers had texted me one word: Ma.

On December 25, 2018, I learned that sometimes, signs can make you feel insane. Other times, they can also be your tie to another reality, another Universe, where you and a loved one can continue your relationship beyond the realm in which we exist now.

It's been four years since my Ma passed. As the months stack against her life and our communication becomes stronger and clearer, I've stopped believing that life ends when your heart stops.

* * *

It's the same with our sweet animals. When they pass, sometimes you think you hear them or maybe feel them. Because it *is* them. Their souls visit us! They are even responsible for sending us our next earth angel pet.

Monica's clients often tell her that they still see and feel their beloved pets. When she tunes into the Other Side, she can see them there as well. They are always with a loved one who has passed, a constant companion even on the Other Side. Cue the waterworks!

Monica

We hear and "see" our sweet Carley (rescued Beagle) all the time. Every time we think of Carley, we will get a sign. A TV commercial with a beagle, an actual beagle with the name of Carley, etc. One night, I came home and pulled into the garage. I opened my door and felt Carley's essence. It caught me off guard. Then, as I was walking into the house, I actually smelled her. I wondered why all of the sudden she was coming in. Well, my husband had just pulled out her pet collar and put it in the garage. She was letting us know she was still with us.

Our beloved loved ones and animal babies are still with us. They will send signs and try to let us know they are still with us. If you ever get a sign and think, "Oh, that was just a coincidence," we are here to tell you that it's not a coincidence but an actual visitation. Please know that you can still talk to them and they can hear you. They are with you at all the special occasions and moments in your life. They might not be here in physical form, but they are here in spiritual form.

CHAPTER 8

Why You Are Here: Your Mission

Mission (n.): *A strongly felt aim, ambition, or calling. From the Latin word mittere meaning "send." Origin: mid-16th century, denoting the sending of the Holy Spirit into the world.*

The Other Side has always told Monica that the key to happiness and peace is living your mission. It's the embodiment of your soul and the fullest expression of you.

We all have a mission that no one else can live for us or fulfill in the way we can. You are the key player in a mission that will help heal, teach, or serve a specific community. Your mission is your legacy.

That is why you have a yearning to do something, to be something, and your life will continue to point you in that direction. It's why you're restless or bored, sad, or even depressed. If you've ever asked, *Is this all there is?* despite having the house, the dog, the kids, the car, the job, the fill-in-the-blank that "they" told you would make you happy, you're probably off mission.

You can be grateful for all of the gifts in your life *and also* yearn for something else. Your mission is that unshakeable feeling that something is still missing. It's your soul trying to get your attention through the noise of external voices and opinions, societal expectations, and norms. If it sounds selfish to go in search of your mission, consider this: being on mission will not only yield more contentment and joy in your life, but it's also how you will best serve the collective.

Your Soul's Assignment

You signed up for your mission before you got here. Before coming to earth, in this body in this lifetime, your soul raised its hand, pointed at the alpaca farm, and said, *I'll take it.*

Or maybe you decided that your mission is to open your home to foster children. Or learn a foreign language so that you can help immigrants. Or sing karaoke every Friday night at the corner bar because the world definitely needs more Donna Summer.

You don't need to be smart or funny or rich or beautiful or talented or whatever you think you're lacking to have a mission. Your mission does not discriminate. There is nothing you can do wrong to not receive a mission, and there is nothing you could do to "mess up" your mission. We all have a mission because it is our birthright. You may wander off course for years or decades. You may be eighty and still searching for your mission, and it will still be waiting for you when you're ready.

Writing this book was part of our mission. Monica was minding her own business, helping clients discover and fulfill their mission, and watching as their lives transformed. She knew she had to share these lessons with a broader audience, but—spoiler alert—Monica hates to write.

Even when her Team kept sending her messages and signs, insisting she write a book, Monica refused. She ultimately struck a deal with her Team: *send me a coauthor and I'll do it.*

At this point, we had been working together for five years. I was on my own mission, hosting a successful podcast and building a virtual marketplace for holistic healers. Even though working with the Other Side had become a way of life and something I talked about ad nauseum at cocktail parties, the thought hadn't occurred to me to write a book about it.

Until the rib dream.

Once we compared notes, the message and our mission were undeniable. From there, the clues kept coming, and our next steps unfolded. We watched in awe (which is saying something) as an agent I had worked with years before, Maria, reached out via Facebook. She was now representing female authors and working with an incredibly talented editor, Johnny. Would I ever consider writing a book?

That editor, Johnny, became our editor. His publisher became our publisher. And a dream team was born along with the book you are holding in your hands.

If it sounds too easy and too good to be true, it is—and it isn't. When you're on mission, the Universe rises up to meet you. When you follow those clues and do your part, the support will show up. When you get stuck, as Monica did with her resistance to writing, the net will appear.

Whatever your soul's intention, the Other Side is standing by to help you make it happen. In our experience, it's not only their mission but their favorite thing to do. Not a bad gig, if you can get it.

Does My Mission Need to Be a Job?

We get this question a lot because our culture is career-obsessed and because we spend so much time working. The answer is no. Missions come in every shape, but they all matter because they all make an impact.

You will make a difference in someone's life or many lives with your mission. You will change the trajectory of the planet with your mission no matter how many people you touch. Your energy will have a ripple effect on the world and humanity.

Your mission doesn't need to be to solve world hunger or write a *New York Times* bestseller (see what we did there). It can be homeschooling the next generation of leaders or brewing kombucha in the basement. You can create TikTok videos for cat lovers or volunteer in your community.

Either way, your mission counts the same.

Your mission is the embodiment of your soul. It does not use the superficial standards of "success" we apply as humans. It does not care what the Joneses are doing or what your parents think. Mission is also the reason there is really no such thing as competition and there is more than enough to go around; all of us are on a specific and different path, even if it looks similar from the outside.

In fact, once you're on mission, those preconceived notions and societal expectations will fade away because they no longer apply to you. They never really did. You'll be so happy and in flow raising those alpacas you will simply not care that LinkedIn doesn't recognize "professional alpaca cuddler" as a job title.

Whether you raise the planet's energy by making people laugh, raise generous human beings, or cure cancer, we all will have an impact on humanity. It is your choice to make a positive impact or a negative one. Making a positive one is not only a lot more fun but also a lot more rewarding. We get back the energy we put out. Choose wisely.

The Greater Reason for Your Mission

Along with your mission, you were assigned a community and a legacy. The Other Side has explained to Monica that every single human being is a part of a bigger puzzle and that we are here to work together. When people realize that they are a specific piece of the puzzle, they will learn to work together. For together is the only way for humans to thrive on earth.

A community is a group of souls that you are here to teach, serve, or heal. It can be your immediate family or friends, neighborhood, or a non-profit you support. It can be a large audience or it can be one person who will go on to change the world because you were assigned to make a difference in their life.

Your mission is designed to have a positive impact and leave a legacy for future generations. Your mission ensures that you accomplish this. By simply being your authentic self, others will benefit indefinitely in ways that may not be apparent or that you may never see or know.

Whatever your mission, it is designed to have a profound ripple effect. The positive impact of your mission, whether it initially touches one person or many, will always extend to the collective.

Consider what happens when you compliment strangers on the street. Their energy instantly shifts. They carry that positivity into their day, and it emanates to everyone they come into contact with. They may start complimenting strangers, too, now that they realize how easy it is to make someone else feel good. All because you spotted a cute teddy coat and said a nice thing.

Now imagine if you spent your life complimenting strangers and you have a glimpse at what is possible. Your mission, whether it's your job or a hobby or how you raise your children, contributes to the collective in a way that only you can.

Why the World Needs You to Be on Mission

The world is an ever-evolving natural and spiritual ecosystem. It's a living organism with elements that are working in conjunction for the betterment of humanity and the planet. Every animal, tree, and body of water has a purpose. Every country, city, and community was also assigned a purpose that only they can provide.

You are the same. You have an important role to contribute to this world. You are the only one who can contribute in this way. It is your very own special mission. Without you, there would be a missing piece in the puzzle. We as a species and a planet suffer when one someone doesn't live his or her mission.

No matter what race, social economical background, familial circumstances, or tragedies that occur in your life, you are here on an important mission and you matter. You are more important than you will ever know. You are here to contribute something amazing for the betterment of humanity. You are here to leave the world a better place. You are here to serve a community. The community can be a neighbor, your family, strangers, causes, your city, your state, your country. No job is too small, and it will always have a ripple effect.

Make the decision to find your mission and serve. That is where peace, happiness, and joy reside.

When You're Off Mission

Sadly, we humans are bombarded with what our lives should look like, how we should look, and what we should be. We are also "given" our definition of success from family, friends, teachers, the media. When we allow this information to direct our lives, we will fall out of alignment with our mission.

When this happens, you could feel sad, anxious, depressed, or stagnant, and life becomes difficult. You may feel like you are on a hamster wheel of despair. And because you are in this state of resistance or low vibration, you will continue to bring more of what's making you feel sad, anxious, and depressed.

No matter what you do, you won't feel happy, peaceful, and fulfilled because it's not your mission. You are studying to be a doctor when you want to be an alpaca farmer. You're miserable because you're chasing someone else's expectation instead of chasing you.

And so the cycle continues, bringing you more despair. Everything is hard because you're not in flow with your life's mission and you are not as happy as you are meant to be because you are not doing what you are meant to be doing.

Can you finish medical school and be a good doctor? Sure. Will you live in joy, peace, and serenity? Probably not. You will continue bringing in moments that cause despair because your soul wants you to course-correct into bliss by being in alignment with your mission.

This is the moment when you get to argue seventeen reasons why you can't drop out of school. You're scared. What will people think? You have student loans to pay. You have no idea what alpacas eat.

We hear you, and we get it. Those reasons are all real, and they are valid. You will come back to them again and again in the course of your life because you're human. But highlight this: the Other Side is prepared to help you navigate each and every reason until the path to your mission is clear.

The beautiful thing is that when you're not on mission, when your life is out of alignment, it will start falling apart. Doors will keep shutting on you. Opportunities won't pan out. Or your life starts to fall apart.

You won't get the job you think you want or the promotion you think you deserve. The person you thought was "the one" will leave. You'll lose your job. A tree will fall on your house (true story). Your back will give out—twice (also true). The other shoe will actually drop.

What appears to be a complete and total breakdown is actually a breakthrough. Call it a dark night of the soul or just a really shitty year, but these moments are trying to move you back into alignment and point you toward your mission.

We urge you to celebrate these moments instead of fearing them or despairing. They are pivots, reshiftings, and openings to get back into alignment. Difficult times provide a pause in life to reevaluate what your soul truly wants, needs, and has undoubtedly been asking for despite your resistance.

You can fight the sea change, you can throw your toys out of the crib, or you can thank the Other Side for guiding you to something better and in your highest good. You don't need to know why, but you do need to trust that, to quote Gabby Bernstein, the Universe has your back. The sooner you allow these seemingly dark moments to pass, the sooner you get to light.

What It Feels Like to Be on Mission

When you're on mission, life flows towards you. You don't struggle. You are at peace, optimistic, and in a joyful state of mind. Everything feels possible. You wake up so happy and can't wait to start your day. Your heart is full because you know you are helping someone. Work doesn't feel like work.

A reward for being on mission is that you don't struggle. You don't spend endless energy chasing things like money, fame, recognition, or unrealistic expectations. What your soul needs comes to you because you are on mission.

When you are helping others, which is inherent to everyone's mission, you are living from a higher vibrational level. This level is where all the good things reside. Because you are living at this level, support appears on its own with no need to chase anything.

You can also tell that you're on mission when every step appears when needed. You might want to write a book but don't know how. You ask the Other Side to send the most amazing person to help you—and they appear! You could need a business partner to expand your work or a web designer to build your new site, and someone will call to give you a name.

When you focus on your mission, life will flow to you in the most magical way. Standing by to assist you in identifying and living your mission is the Other Side. In the next chapters, you'll learn how to enlist them to identify and embrace your mission. Get excited!

CHAPTER 9

Discovering Your Mission

Your only purpose is to be yourself,
otherwise you deprive the universe
of who you came here to be.

—ANITA MOORJANI

In this chapter, we'll show you how to work with the Other Side to live on mission. You'll apply the lessons from previous chapters to cultivate your mission and begin experiencing the peace that being in alignment brings.

Before we begin, though, we want to provide you with a disclaimer about missions: just like you, they are ever evolving. A mission is not a destination but a way of being. How it looks and manifests will change over time, but the spirit of your mission and its purpose of serving others and leaving a legacy will remain the same.

You Already Know Your Mission

Your body, mind, and soul along with your circumstances will always point you toward your mission. It is imperative that you know this so you can start paying attention to yourself and your life.

Only you, with the help of your Team, can determine your mission. When we start living on autopilot or allowing others to dictate our lives, our priorities, values, and choices, or our way of being, we become misaligned with our mission.

Life will then become difficult. It's how the Other Side wakes you up and tries to reorient you in the right direction. Your Team is always conspiring for you, not against you. These beautiful aspects of yourself are all working together to make sure you have a beautiful, peaceful, and joyful life. All you have to do is listen.

Signs are everywhere about your mission. From the minute you are born to the minute you go back. Your Team never leaves you and is always bringing you your next step.

When Monica does readings and tells people their mission, they always look back and can see the signs. Your mission isn't some big mystery; you may already know what it is but, for all of the reasons we've discussed, are blocking or resisting it.

Your mission always begins with your loves, passions, and desires. What do you love doing? What are you most interested in? What did you want to study (not what your parents wanted you to study)? What did you play when you were little? Did you love to play the teacher or play dress-up? Did you love books, sci-fi films, drawing cartoons, building forts, caring for stray animals, TV/film, the arts or the sciences? Look at your past and take inventory of the things that came naturally to you that you loved and that you wanted to know more about.

You can also look back and see if you received recurring messages from other people. Was there something several people have said that you are good at? Have others repeatedly told you about your particular strengths? Did you win awards for your photography or public service growing up? Always look for themes in your life, for they will provide insight into your mission.

Finally, is there a subject or skill you continuously ponder? Many change-makers in history had a burning question they were trying to solve. Composers, artists, and writers often wondered about something in their craft that drove them to create. They followed that question and fell into their mission. Pay attention to a nagging thought, dream, or feeling, and the Other Side will lead you to your next step.

When doors open for you without effort, it is another sign that you are on the right track. When life flows easily, and your next steps, opportunities, partners, or resources present themselves to you without much work, trust that you are on the right path. Your job is to pay attention and keep going!

Sarah

Sarah was an executive who had graduated from top schools with honors. Her family was full of achievers. She felt she, too, had to super achieve. She had a very coveted, high-paying job at a Fortune

500 company and the kind of beautiful life that most people only dream about.

One day, Sarah noticed that she was "checking out" during a meeting. She realized she was dreading going to work. She dug deeper and realized that she was starting to not feel fulfilled by her job. She was stunned and unsure where all this was coming from.

In a session with Monica, Sarah told Monica that she had been fighting her feelings of wanting to be a stay-at-home mother for years. She felt guilty because she had worked so hard to get where she was and most people would kill for her job. In her heart, Sarah knew she was supposed to stay home with her babies but didn't know how.

During the session, her Team confirmed that family and children were a huge part of Sarah's mission. In fact, they were at the top of her list. When Monica shared this mission with her, she let out a huge sigh, and Monica could literally feel her shoulders drop.

When COVID-19 hit, she was able to stay home and finally realized that her heart was staying home with her kids. Once the decision was made, all of her angst, anxiety, and lack of fulfillment lifted. She is thrilled being a stay-at-home mom and is thriving.

Begin Where You Are

We've talked about how being off mission can affect everything from your mental and/or physical health to your relationships to your quality of life. The sooner you begin to align with your soul's calling, the sooner you will shift to a place of peace and contentment. That's why you're never too old—or too young—to start your mission. The invitation never expires.

Monica's client booked a session for her eleven-year-old son. They asked the Team to identify his gifts and mission.

The answers astonished him; they were everything he wanted to be and do. Unfortunately, his father had other ideas. Like many parents, he was projecting his desires and dreams onto his child because he hadn't fulfilled his own. Now, his son was more determined than ever to not allow others' opinions to determine his path in life. You could feel his joy and relief because the Other Side had validated what he was here to do. We can't wait to watch him grow up and set an example for others to live their mission!

Your Mission Is Always Evolving

Another client, a very young eighty-seven-year-old who had spent her time living her mission, was being pressured by her family to retire. She wasn't ready and came to Monica asking for guidance. Her Team told her it wasn't time yet, and her mission took another turn. Although she had worked with all adults during her career, the Other Side sent her signs to volunteer with youth. They even told her it could be once a month or once a week. She got to choose. She said that she kept feeling she was supposed to work with children but had no idea how. She was over the moon that she would be helping the future generation and to have a renewed purpose.

Mission Control: Asking Your Team for Guidance

Remember, you have a beautiful spiritual team that never leaves your side and whose main job is to help you! They signed up for this and are just sitting there waiting for you to send an SOS.

In previous chapters, we shared how to work with your Team for guidance on everything from finding a parking spot to moving to a new city. The process is the same for getting aligned with your mission.

Start by taking the pressure off of yourself. This is a marathon, not a sprint, and while our idea of an endurance sport is binge-watching *Real Housewives*, we strongly encourage you to settle in for the journey. Approach your mission with curiosity, not urgency or panic. Neither will yield authentic or immediate answers. Pop some popcorn. Get cozy. And get excited. You're about to engage your Team on their most important assignment yet: helping you remember who you are.

So, like, there are these friendly wizards who sit around all day waiting for me to tell them what I want to do with my life so they can make it happen?

Yes, and you also have to do the work. When you're ready to find and fulfill your mission, follow these steps. The more open you are to receiving the Other Side's support and guidance, the faster it will come in.

1. Acknowledge your Team, let them know how thankful you are for them, and grant them permission to help you.
2. Ask your Team to send you the same sign three times within three days regarding the next step in your mission. Notice we said step. You may not receive your mission in blazing lights or wrapped with a bow. More often, you'll receive steps that build

on one another, leading to your mission. For example: a course to take, book to read, subject matter to explore.

3. Affirm to your Team that you need to be hit over the head with the sign so you know it's from them.

Repeat as needed. Continue to ask your Team for signs as you navigate and embrace your mission. As you begin to live it, your mission will evolve with you. While your core purpose remains constant, it will take on different forms as you master it.

Your work is never done, nor is your Team's!

Common Fears Around Taking the Leap

It is very common when finding your mission that fears will arise. Monica has seen clients who have degrees in different fields than their mission. There are also people who want to leave their high-paying job to be stay-at-home mothers. Both of us left stable careers to live our mission, and, despite the upheaval to our identities and insecurity of the unknown, taking the leap has been one of our greatest joys.

Some people have judgment and shame tied to what they do with their lives or changes required to align with their mission. There are all types of fears that might come up for you when discovering your mission. That is okay. It is completely normal.

If fears arise, sit with them. Don't judge or run from them. Your fear is real, but the more you allow it to just be, the less power it will have over you. Do not just write off your mission because it makes you anxious or frightened. Processing is always the best way to move through a fear. Really look at the fear, and once broken down, you will see that it is unnecessary.

Remember that beginning the journey to be on mission is not all-or-nothing. Start with one step at a time, and be patient!

The Other Side often talks about a "bridge job" for people whose mission involves a career change. If you need income while in the discovery phase, take a job that allows you to start your process of mission on the side or, if it's an option, restructure your current job to support your exploration.

You might begin by taking a class that interests you, reading books, listening to a podcast on your desired subject, or even taking a fun class to lift your spirits up.

Again, this process is one step at a time. It's not meant to be laborious. On the contrary, this is meant to be fun, rewarding, and fascinating. You know you are on mission when your steps are meaningful, fun, peaceful, and joyous.

When Your Mission Doesn't Go as "Planned"

First, set aside any expectations of what your mission or the steps to find it will look like—or how long it will take. That is not your job.

Your desires are important—they are clues into your mission—but the shape they take is a mystery that it's not our job as humans to control. You might think you know best, but no one knows what will bring you into alignment better than your Team. If you continue to ask the Other Side for guidance, you'll never be off course.

The Universe and your spiritual team are miraculous beings. They are constantly working on our behalf. They love to step in and course-correct when needed. Never feel that something didn't go as planned or that you took a "wrong" turn. Everything will and can be used to assist you on your journey and mission. Nothing you do is wasted or a waste of time.

Try to view perceived setbacks, disappointments, or hardships as experiences that can be used to serve you or your community that you are here to help. Your role is to keep moving forward. To recenter, regroup, and realign when these things happen. No need to despair. Remember, we get to choose the emotion we establish to the event. Choose to see things in a positive perspective, and positivity will come out of it and back to you.

If your mission is not moving along the way you want, if you find yourself frustrated with the process or the timeline or are still being met with resistance, or if you're following the steps and it still doesn't feel good, take a break.

Mission work is not for the faint of heart. It is the ultimate faith and trust walk with both yourself and the Other Side. Sometimes, stepping away and just living your life provides the clarity and calm you need to continue on your path.

Your Team will never give up on you. They are committed and they are persistent!

CHAPTER 10

Mission Realignment: Embracing Setbacks

As humans, we worry about big, disruptive changes like job loss, breakups, divorce, financial losses, and friendship fallouts. We've been conditioned to perceive these challenges as setbacks, when in reality they are divine guidance in action.

The Other Side wants us to reframe the way we perceive and categorize such events in our lives. It's their way of leading us and course-correcting for us when we drift from whatever is in our highest good. Setbacks are the Other Side's attempt to nudge you toward your next step, circumstances, or people that will change your life for the better.

When massive change or disappointment occurs, you are being moved to your next phase because the current one no longer serves you. You are being repositioned for something (or someone) that's a better fit for the person you're here to be. You are being realigned with your soul and your mission. You're being realigned with YOU.

Perceived setbacks are a move forward, not backwards. They are an opportunity to learn a lesson so that you can continue chasing you.

Take job loss, as we know that's the change many people fear most. How many times have you been despondent about losing a job or not getting the position you were interviewing for only to land one later that was a much better fit, with higher pay, or with a nicer boss? The Other Side may have even put you through the first interview process to meet the recruiter who will someday think of you for your dream job. They will bring you exactly what you need, especially if you're willing to have faith—and patience.

Put Down the Backpack

Rather than approaching such unwanted changes with despair, the Other Side wants us to get curious and ask, "Where is this taking me?" or "What are you trying to teach me?"

Easier said than done because you're only human and the disappointment is real. We could tell you that a job loss or breakup is a gift (because it is), but when you're in it, it feels more like a box of sh*t tied up with a bow just for you.

If you're going to freak out, then freak out. If you need to cry, cry it out. But only do it for ten to twenty minutes. Then get still. Any longer and you'll be operating from a lower vibration of despair. This is like wearing a heavy backpack and expecting to climb a mountain effortlessly.

Monica often tells clients: DO NOT PUT ON THE BACKPACK. Try a fanny pack (so hot right now) or cross-body bag instead. Anything but a backpack. You are better able to receive the Other Side's clues and signs when you're not trudging up that mountain in the fog carrying a forty-pound pack of pain and Flaming Hot Cheetos.

So allow yourself to grieve. Get angry. Scream into a pillow. Eat all the ice cream. Throw the pity party. But don't stay too long, because the sooner you move through the breakdown, the sooner you get to the breakthrough.

When an unwanted change occurs, look for patterns. Are you always losing your job because you, in fact, dread what you're doing but are too afraid to follow your soul's calling? Then it's time to heal the pattern and release the limiting beliefs that are holding you back from doing something different.

Do you tend to attract codependent or unsupportive partners? Don't be surprised when relationships continue to end. The Other Side will keep giving you opportunities to heal and learn the lesson because once you do, you'll be ready for a healthier partnership.

Your job loss, financial worries, or relationship changes are opportunities for growth—and something better. If you can view them with gratitude and curiosity, you're ready to cocreate a way forward with your Team that will bring more joy and peace.

Katie

Monica's client, Katie, had worked with her Team and was tuned into their messages. More importantly, she had learned to trust in her inner voice.

So when Katie found herself driving around the Yucca Valley, California with a friend, looking at potential rental properties to buy, she knew was coming face to face with the next step of her mission.

She could picture herself renovating and redecorating houses there. She could feel her hands in the desert dirt doing yardwork. She belonged there. The vision was so strong, it was as if it were already a reality. The how wasn't important. Katie trusted that this would present itself.

At the time, Katie was doing completely different work. She had been at her corporate product-management job for more than three years in an industry that she cared about. Although she didn't feel wildly connected to the work, she enjoyed her coworkers and had deep gratitude for the financial stability that the job afforded. After years of running her own business, it was the first time in her life she didn't have to worry about money.

But she *had* started to miss being an entrepreneur and the autonomy and creativity that comes from working for yourself. At the same time, Katie couldn't envision a business that wouldn't involve major risk, fundraising, and hustling. She had been there, done that, and didn't want to do it again. She valued her steady paycheck too much.

The Other Side had other ideas.

One month after closing on her first house in the desert, Katie's company announced a reorg and eliminated her position. Instead of being disappointed, she was relieved because the decision had been made *for* her (THANKS, TEAM).

Katie had purchased the first house with a business partner before she had lost her job. Although she had intended to rent it out as a low-pressure side gig, she was now beginning to think that it could be more. It could become a business.

She had never owned a house or had equity in anything. The idea of investing in more real estate that would appreciate in value appealed to her need for security, while getting to renovate and marketing the property checked the boxes for using her creativity and business savvy. And, because vacation rentals were a known quantity, managing them wouldn't require her to reinvent the wheel.

And yet.

Katie still looked for a new job. She took some recruiter calls and went to a few interviews but was only going through the motions. If she was honest with herself, the idea of doing the same thing while having to start over at a new company filled her with dread.

Instead, she decided to take her severance, unemployment, and savings and bought a second house. It was a risk, but instead of focusing on that, she chose to focus on how much joy her new business would bring.

Katie now feels like she's living her purpose. She nerds out on baseboards and paint colors. She loves the challenge of landscaping in the desert and creating beautiful spaces for her renters.

It's still a long game. She may need to take a side gig until the properties generate a livable profit, but in Katie's words, *It is all worth it.*

EXERCISE: Getting Realigned

The same method you used in Chapter 5 to ask for signs applies to working with the Other Side to overcome setbacks with purpose and self-compassion.

Once you've grounded your emotions and gotten still, call in your Team. Grant them permission to help you and go into conversation with them.

If you're ready to take action, ask for next steps. If you want to better understand the situation and how you got here, ask for clarity. If you've identified a frustrating pattern and are ready to break the cycle, ask for guidance. Above all, trust yourself and what you need help with to move forward.

Sample questions for your Team:

- *What is my next step to move forward?*
- *Why is this change occurring?*
- *What is this event trying to teach me?*
- *What can I learn from it?*
- *What do I need to heal in order to stop repeating this pattern?*

Then let it go and allow your Team to show you your next step. The signs will start appearing, and, more importantly, you'll be able to identify them IF you allow yourself to stay in a place of positive energy. Remember, this setback is a gift. Celebrate that you are being moved up, that you're learning a lesson, and that you're being moved forward to meet the right partner or find the right opportunity. If you slip back into worry, fear, or—even worse—blaming yourself for the situation, it will be very difficult to clearly see what's right in front of you.

The signs and guidance can come in through a visual symbol, physical object, or flash of insight. For example, a person's name suddenly pops into your head or someone you haven't spoken to in ages "randomly" reaches out for a coffee date. Follow those breadcrumbs because they could be a teacher, messenger, or opportunity for you.

You could also receive signs to further your education or explore a new subject matter.

For example, you could be listening to a podcast that a friend sent you on the making of *Star Wars* and, that same day, find an email in your inbox inviting you to a panel discussion with film directors. While walking the dog that afternoon, you pass someone wearing a Skywalker Ranch hat. Maybe you're just a Star Wars superfan, or maybe it's time to finally research a career in the movie industry.

Or let's say you're a foodie who's gotten really into curing meats on the weekend (as one does) when a new butcher shop opens down the street—and needs weekend help. You ignore it until you overhear the person sitting next you on the subway raving about the pastrami sandwich they had for lunch.

There are some signs even an algorithm can't make up. They are your Team's way of nudging you back into alignment. Call them in, ask for guidance, and they will move mountains, people, and even charcuterie to deliver the message.

The Other Side is always standing by to help. But remember, you are in 50/50 partnership with them. It's *your* job to keep your energy high, pay attention, and trust the process. They'll provide the signs; you provide the action.

CHAPTER 11

Bless It or Block It

The Other Side is always trying to help you. There are times when they need you to step aside so they can do their job. When you don't step aside, you can get in the way of your intended path.

If you struggle with delegation or relinquishing control, this will either be your favorite chapter or worst nightmare.

When you try to control everything, you leave no room for what you need, only what you *think* you want. When you hold on loosely, you leave room for the unexpected, for surprise and delight. What if the outcome is better than you could've imagined?

Surrendering to the Other Side is the ultimate faith and trust walk. It's also one of the surest paths to peace. The more you resist, the harder it is for your Team to help you and for you to receive their guidance. But when you let go and allow the Other Side to do its thing, solutions present themselves. You next step is revealed, and life flows.

This is especially true when you are trying to make a big decision or meeting resistance on something you want, for example, weighing a job offer, cross-country move, or whether a third date is a good or terrible idea. If you're unsure of what to do or are being met with resistance in some area of your life, the Other Side asks two things: release any expectations or attachments to the outcome and use the *bless-it-or-block-it* method.

Asking the Other Side to *bless it or block it* will allow you to let go of the outcome. And being attached to an outcome is a big no-no for the Other Side because it ties our energy up in something that may or may not be for us. Remember, the Other Side knows what's in your highest good.

We won't pretend that the faith and trust walk we're asking of you is easy. As recovering Type A personalities, this concept is still crazy making for us at times. But it's crucial to receiving what the Other Side wants to provide. The tremendous peace you'll experience when you bless it or block it is worth it—as is the relief you'll feel when you realize that by giving it up to your Team, you dodged a bullet or two.

Using this method for travel is a great way to test it and flex your trust muscle. Missed connection? Watch yourself get upgraded on the next flight. Trying to plan a beach vacation with friends and you can't agree on dates? Bless it or block it and avoid a hurricane the week you wanted to go. Even taking a wrong turn can be the Other Side blocking you from a traffic jam down the road.

Monica

I was planning our annual international family trip. We were supposed to tour Greece. Every single time I went to plan it with my travel agent, something would happen. We couldn't get hotels, the flights weren't working out, the tours we wanted wouldn't be available...and on and on. I had never had so many issues planning a trip before. I pushed through because my family really wanted to go, even though I knew the Other Side was blocking it for some inexplicable reason. I kept telling my husband, "I don't think we're supposed to go."

I finally settled on an okay trip, even though it wasn't the one I had envisioned, and on a whim added travel insurance, which we never do. (Who does?) Good thing I listened to the Other Side because the following week, COVID-19 hit and we couldn't travel anywhere.

* * *

Your Team will block anything that can hinder your progress or any doors you're not supposed to walk through to get you back on track. They can see steps, streets, and even years ahead and will place you in the right place at the right time with the right people accordingly—if you let them block it or bless it.

If something is meant to be to help you in any way and the timing is right, *it will happen.* But you have to trust that whatever the outcome, it is *for* you. The Other Side asks us to use the energetic statement of *bless it or block it* to move out of the way and allow them to lead you.

The Other Side wants to get you from point A to point B in the straightest line possible so that you can be in flow and on mission. As humans we sometimes like to take the scenic route because we aren't ready for the fast lane (see: fears, insecurities), and that's okay. However, the Other Side will block anything that takes you on the scenic route, even if there are Instagrammable views and a roadside diner that serves really good pie. This is one of those times when the direct route is way more fun!

When you obsess about or focus on an outcome and it doesn't go your way, the disappointment can derail you from your path or, at the very least, cause extreme Ben & Jerry's consumption. You may even think you did something wrong, or worse, that you're being punished. Any of these reactions can lead to despair, anxiety, or panic, when in fact, the Other Side was protecting you and has something better in store.

We've talked a lot about blocking, but the Other Side also blesses anything that will benefit you in some way. Even if it's a stepping stone, they will bless it. Anything or anyone that provides us soul growth lessons will also be blessed. If you ask for something and it comes your way, walk through that door. It will provide some type of benefit now or in the future.

The next time you find yourself at a crossroads in your career, are waiting for those three little dots to appear after your last date with McDreamy, or are debating whether Coachella with your coworkers is wise, say it with us: *bless it or block it.*

Put it on a Post-it. Tell a friend. Hashtag it all you want. We'd TM it if we could. Then step away and accept the outcome no matter what it is. Just saying or writing those words—*bless it or block it*—will put you in a state of surrender and allow the Other Side do its job.

Let them decide what's in your best interest. They'll either give you the thumbs up or shut it down. If you don't get the job, the date, the campsite, it wasn't meant to be. If you do, you can trust that it's for you.

Samantha

A marketing executive in her late forties, Samantha lost her job unexpectedly. She had been at the company for two years and loved the work as well as the people. She was blindsided to be let go and felt betrayed, hurt, and utterly disposed of by the leadership. It was as if the rug had been pulled out from underneath her. It broke her heart to leave, and she had no idea what to do next.

At the same time, if she was honest with herself, she had been struggling with burnout and frustration at the job. Earlier, she had been passed over for a promotion and didn't feel supported by her new boss. She had that nagging feeling that she couldn't grow at the company, that the environment was becoming toxic and affecting her wellbeing. Samantha had a nagging feeling that she needed to make a change but wasn't ready to give up.

The Universe had other plans.

Finding a new job was a full-time job and an emotional one. Samantha applied for more than sixty positions and interviewed for a dozen roles. She met with recruiters and hired an executive coach. The networking calls and coffees were endless.

After three months putting in more than forty hours a week on her search and freelancing on the side, Samantha had hit only dead ends. Every day brought another rejection and countless Tootsie Rolls consumed. The hardest ones were when her resume checked every box on the job description.

Well into her job search, Samantha knew what industries and type of work she wanted to do. When an opportunity finally came up after twenty hours of interviews with eleven people, she felt relieved to have found a job but didn't love that the work itself wasn't interesting or exciting. She knew she should be grateful for the opportunity and wanted to stay open, but taking the job felt off on a soul level. But who was she to turn it down?

Samantha asked her Team to bless it or block it. She let the Other Side decide what was in her highest good.

Within days, Samantha got two other offers. They were vastly different opportunities, including one she hadn't even applied for. Empowered by her options, she was very upfront with both potential employers about her requirements. She wanted a role and a company that supported work/life balance and her mental health, development opportunities, the option to work from home and set her own schedule, a salary that supported her family. She was open and honest about what she needed.

Again, she asked the Other Side to bless it or block it. If it was for her, the right job would reveal itself.

In the end, both employers met her requests, but Samantha took the job that was most aligned with her mission of supporting marginalized communities. Her new CEO was committed to social justice and using his influence and resources for good. It seemed the Other Side had been connecting the dots for her all along.

Samantha says that a huge part of this experience has been finally admitting that her career has been one of her only sources of self-worth. Since she was a kid, accolades and critiques of her performance at school and work had dictated how Samantha felt about herself. She translated getting let go from her job as "You are not enough, you should be ashamed of yourself" in the loudest, most devastating way. She is now working with her Team to find self-worth outside of her job, making space in life for the experiences, people, and places that they put forward and redefining what success and happiness mean to her.

When No Means Not Right Now

Bless it or block it is always subject to divine timing. Don't give up hope if there's something you want that's been blocked. Have faith that the Other Side knows what it's doing. If it's for you, it will come around again—when the time is right.

Let's say you dream of being a Dallas Cowboys cheerleader. Just because you don't make the cut on your first tryout doesn't mean you never will. Maybe it was blocked because you need more time to practice your technique to avoid injury. Or a family member is going to need your help in the year ahead and you wouldn't have time otherwise. Or maybe you're about to get a once-in-a-lifetime opportunity to volunteer overseas that wouldn't have been possible if you'd committed to cheering.

No is not always the final answer. Sometimes *not right now* is the Other Side's way.

CHAPTER 12

Getting Still

In addition to receiving signs from your Team, you can also receive messages in moments of stillness. You know that phrase *I can't hear myself think?* The same goes for the Other Side. They are always speaking to us, but we have to slow down long enough to hear them. Finding stillness will aid in your ability to hear and receive their messages as well as access your inner knowing.

As much as you may find yourself talking to your Team while in the drive-through at In-N-Out, the quickest way to receive their help is by getting still. Completely still. Alone still. No devices or distractions still.

Creating a stillness practice is the best way we know how. The goal is to create a sacred time and place to be still. This can be in your home, favorite chair, outdoors, in a garden, park, even in your car. Some find it helpful to use the same place every day. Find what works for you. Once you've established the space, be sure you can be present here without distractions—including pets and especially kids!

This is your sacred time and place. You can use it to meditate, pray, contemplate, create, or ask your Team for answers. You can practice for five minutes or for however long the spirit moves you. There is no one-size-fits-all. The secret is to use the time wisely. Your stillness practice is like a magical container in which you can connect with yourself and the Other Side for guidance.

Make space during your practice to:

- *Read—what interests you.*
- *Think—about your life.*
- *Ponder—what is right in your life? What would you like to be different?*
- *Create—anything.*
- *Review—your life, your schedule, where you are spending your time, and where you are spending your energy.*
- *Revaluate—when faced with challenges or difficulties.*
- *Refuel—nourish, nap, or do nothing.*
- *Recharge—in any way that energizes you. Nature is amazing for this.*
- *Contemplate—what you are feeling, without judgment.*
- *Nurture - yourself, your dreams, your life.*
- *Dream—about your wishes and desires.*
- *Get curious—about what excites, interests, or fills you up.*
- *Be in awe—of your experiences, lessons, and the person you are becoming.*

- *Be in gratitude—for this moment of stillness and your connection to Spirit.*

Being in the present moment will allow you to hear your Team's directional guidance. This guidance will come in the form of answers, steps, or flashes of insight. Most of the time, it will sound like your own voice. It will not come in the form of lightning crashing and a loud booming voice coming down from on high (unless you're Monica).

You'll wonder where you got the thought or idea because it will just come to you. Don't question it; this guidance is coming from your Team. It's your job to follow the advice that comes in. If you are not ready to act on the guidance, then write it down so you can revisit later. You will know when it is time to act on it.

Please note that the Other Side only speaks through love. Their messages will always be worded in a positive or constructive way. They will not use harsh words, negative thoughts, or self-talk. Your Team won't ever tell you that you're fat, a failure, or not enough. They'll say, "It's time to start moving your body in a beautiful and fun way!" or "Why don't you reach out to that new contact for a coffee date?" That said, if they tell you something with urgency—e.g., to leave a toxic situation or relationship—it's worth heeding.

Practicing stillness daily is ideal, if not imperative, for both your spiritual connection and inner peace. However, start where you can, even if it's just once a week. You'll soon look forward to this time and the restorative and energizing benefits.

CHAPTER 13

Kids and the Other Side

We all come into the world with a Team. Kids are even more tuned into theirs because they haven't been as jaded by society yet. They are born innately trusting themselves and the Other Side. The sooner you teach them how to tap in, the sooner they can start receiving guidance and develop the confidence to be their authentic self and discover their mission. They won't have to spend so much of their adulthood chasing. They will also be less likely to feel alone in the world or fear being different or less than.

When introducing your kids to the Other Side, use the same steps that we outlined in Chapter 5, which Monica initially developed for her own children. You can wait until you get the hang of them yourself, or you can learn them as a family. Just as you might read the *Harry Potter* series together, there is magic in sharing the experience. You know best what age your kids are ready to meet their Team.

Step One: Acknowledge their Team

They can call in each group (angels, spirit guides, etc.) individually or group them together as the Team. Have them thank their Team for being with them and grant them permission to help them. This step makes for a sneaky bonus lesson in manners and gratitude!

Step Two: Ask their Team for the same sign three times within three days

Explain to your kiddo that the signs can come from physical objects such as a feather, coin, or butterfly. They can also come in as a picture of the object, like a game piece, license plate, sticker on a car, billboard, social media, article, movie, illustration, or even from someone else. Let them know if they only receive two signs, then they might have missed the third one just as adults sometimes do. Kids tend to turn this step into a treasure hunt, so reinforce that they needn't go looking for the signs but allow themselves to be surprised. Another way to present this step is as gifts or clues from the Other Side.

Step Three: Affirm to their Team that they need to please make sure they see the sign

This way their Team will try their hardest to help your child see the sign.

We encourage you to start with something small in the beginning. Your child could ask for a coin, favorite animal, or other familiar object. Once the magic occurs, they will have an immediate connection to the Other Side and the realization that they do exist and are standing by for a spiritual play date. Once kids meet their Team, the experience is with them forever.

After they have started with something small, they can continue using the steps for other questions or guidance. Let's say your child has to make a decision between two sports or activities. They could ask their Team to send them the same sign three times within three days on what team or club to sign up for. See AJ's story about the school mascot!

CHAPTER 14

More Stories from the Other Side

If you've made it to this point in the book and implemented the exercises we've outlined, then you know the Other Side exists and is eager to assist you on your mission. Even so, it's natural to question whether what you're experiencing is real. It's human nature to question what seems too good to be true, and real talk: we are completely guilty of it as well, even after all of the magic we've witnessed.

That's when hearing the stories of people (besides us) who have walked this path can provide reassurance that a) you're not crazy, b) you're not imagining the messages you're receiving, and c) it's safe to trust them. If you jumped ahead to get to the tea, well then, may this chapter inspire you to revisit the lessons and put them into practice for yourself.

The following individuals generously offered up their very personal journeys with the Other Side to further inspire you to embark on your own. Like us, they know what's possible when you invite in your Team and want you to enjoy the same purpose and peace that working with them brings.

Jen

I know that I am never alone. My Team is always supporting and guiding me. Until I met Monica, I didn't take the guidance seriously or comprehend that it was coming from my Team. Once I started to pay more attention and follow the signs, life became pretty magical.

My Team has shown me how they work with me. For example, one time I was texting my dog's vet to "please prescribe meds for Milo's diarrhea so he doesn't keep me up all night."

But the text wouldn't send. The app kept crashing until I stopped and asked my Team, "What am I doing wrong?"

Right away, the answer popped into my head: *You are creating energy with your words!*

I rewrote the text, removing the line about Milo keeping me up all night, and, sure enough, it sent.

My Team was teaching me how to shift my energy and attitude. This is just one example of how my guides teach me—and have a sense of humor!

Life is now a pretty constant conversation with my Team. I receive daily guidance from the Other Side that keeps me on the right path in little and big ways. From a gut feeling that I need to go to a certain store, only to receive a beautiful inspirational message from someone there (unknowingly to them) or find an item I have been wanting for a long time, to a feeling that I need to call someone without knowing the reason (only to discover it when I do), there are so many ways I am constantly guided now that I have made an effort to notice and purposely connect with my Team and divine guidance. I don't react quickly anymore like I used to—I always check in with them first. I always ask for clarity. I watch that what I do and say is in alignment with what I want for my life and comes from a place of love.

Charlotte

My life has drastically changed for the better since the minute I met Monica and was introduced to the Other Side. I have received undeniable support from my Team in the form of countless moments of synchronicity, from song lyrics on the radio guiding me at the exact moment I needed them to butterflies in unlikely places.

The major life changes that have taken place since understanding my connection to the Other Side were deep wishes that I felt a lot of uncertainty around, including a baby on the way and a dream home that feels like it came out of the sky.

For more than a year, we looked for a house in a very tough market, and every single property that I thought I wanted, we did not get. I always accepted the tough losses, trusting Monica's guidance to *bless it or block it* as I tried to find the best fit for our family. When an extraordinarily unique home came on the market that was the perfect match for our personal history and preferences, it turned out to be the one.

During this process, I was yearning for another child but wasn't sure it would happen. On moving day, of all days, we conceived this child. It was as if this child was waiting to enter into this new peaceful space. Everything feels spiritually linked. When we were new to the home, I would see cardinals flutter by. I have not seen them since but believe they are loved ones who have passed on, wishing us well in this new chapter.

Never in a million years would I have thought that either of these miracles would come to fruition, but once I understood the magic and power of cocreating with the Other Side, my wishes began to manifest. I am absolutely certain that the nudges and signs I received along the way from my Team were guiding me to these wonderful changes.

Martha

Music has always been a part of my life. Although my parents' advice and my own practicality kept me from turning music into a career, it remains part of my identity in ways that, depending on the decade, float somewhere between serious hobby and semi-professional.

Upon the birth of my second child, I was enveloped in the haze of sleepless nights, maternity leave days, and primal maternal instincts. One was the desire to nurture myself, so that I could remain both strong and sane for my babies. I needed to find a way to get music back into my life, and I became convinced that doing so required finding a studio space outside the home.

I strapped on my new little baby and trolled the streets of our historic downtown, seeking "For Rent" signs in every window. Sadly, our downtown's quaintness translated into very pricy rent rates and landlords who were unwilling to rent to a musician whose music (even a cello) might bother neighboring tenants through shared floors and walls.

My meandering eventually led me to the edge of the commercial district, where I happened upon a sad-looking building that had recently been vacated by a laundromat pick-up and drop-off site whose window signage still boasted, "Drop Your Pants Here!"

I cupped my hands and looked through the full-height storefront window, gently squishing my wriggling Baby Björn against the glass. Inside was an unexpected sight: warm, wood-paneled walls, a sunlit room, and a string of spotlights, which, to me, looked like the perfect space for intimate music practice, rehearsals, and performance.

I was suddenly startled by a man standing right behind me saying, "Would you like to see the space? I own it and could let you in."

I immediately knew it was a sign.

The impromptu tour told me everything I needed to know. It was perfect. I signed a lease a few days later, thinking that the financial hit of this impulsive decision might, at best, be the answer to my call and, at worst, temper it with a hard dose of reality. But within days, my sister alerted me to a flash furniture sale. I felt like I was being led by an outside force that had gathered up the perfect lamps, tables, chairs—everything I needed to outfit the entire space with hip yet functional mid-century modern pieces for less than $700.

Shortly after setting up the place, I held an open house. Like an angel appearing out of nowhere, a local banjo instructor stopped by to see if she could rent the place out some time. Shortly thereafter, a luthier needed space for her workshop. A puppeteer inquired about using the space for his productions. I stopped by a local gallery, where the featured artist had included in his bio a note that he was seeking studio space in town. I called the number, and, within a day, I had another renter and walls decked out in original art. A healthy crowd showed up at every Sunday Jazz Jam, dropping fives and tens and twenties into our donation bowl to help keep the lights on.

Over the next few months, my little studio flourished—to the point that, when we found out the owners wanted to sell, we felt it could work to buy the building. But purchasing and managing commercial property also seemed like a big financial commitment and uncharacteristic leap. Just as potential buyers were beginning to take interest, we received a cash gift from a family member that confirmed for me the building was meant to be ours.

Six years later, Hot Spot Music, "your local music incubator," is an ongoing success beloved by the community. Not only have I found my happy place, an intimate practice studio for my own musical endeavors, but I have shared it with others who feel the same way.

Tammy

Over the years, Monica helped me clear blocks related to family of origin and divorce. Through this continual clearing came a growth of my psychic abilities. The more I worked with my Team, the more my psychic side expanded.

During this time, I found myself drawn to missing person stories in the news. I realized I had an ability to access details about these cases. At the same time, my relationship with my Team was getting stronger, and communication from them was becoming clearer. Instead of simply asking my Team for help, I began asking more specific questions and receiving signs as answers.

It was exciting, but what was I supposed to do with this newfound psychic ability? I knew my Team was helping me when I received an email introducing a new class called Forensic Mediumship. I was shocked; I had never heard of such a class. I did not know what a Medium was but knew I had been doing psychic work in missing person cases, and the class description seemed to fit. With tears streaming down my face, I signed up for the class. I felt my Team had heard me asking for direction, and clearly, this was my next step.

As soon as I signed up for the class, imposter syndrome set in. What if I couldn't do it? What if I had been imagining my gifts? As doubts crept in, I was reminded of the lessons Monica had taught me: discernment over ego, positivity over negativity, connect to the Other Side daily.

Emboldened with positive thoughts and reminders the Team was with me, I traveled to the event. Feeling nervous, I picked a seat toward the back of the room. This would be the first time my ability would be shared publicly.

When the class began, we were grouped with people sitting around us. Unbeknownst to me, I had sat in the middle of four ladies who knew each other and were happy to support a newbie. My nervousness continued to melt away as my contributions to the list of evidence grew. I was connecting! I could feel information flowing! I smiled, thanking my Team for support and finding me the perfect seat.

I left that class having signed up for a Beta group that would create leads on missing person cases for law enforcement. Also, one of the women in the group invited me to join a Mediumship practice. Clearly, my Team had intervened in more ways than one.

I now work as a Psychic/Medium and Reiki Master. My Team continues to help me grow, and I am grateful for their enduring love and guidance.

Manisha

Several years ago, my dog, a Yorkie mix, was diagnosed with a health condition, and I was devastated. The prognosis was positive if managed with conventional medication, but he would have to be on it for the rest of his life. From my own research, I found this regimen could lead to other health complications in old age. I felt in my heart that there had to be another way we could care for our animal.

I continued to talk to my Team every day, asking them to show me the way. In the meantime, we started the medication. One day, out of nowhere, I got an intuitive hit to look up veterinary Chinese medicine in our city. Did that even exist? I didn't know, but I did a quick Google search and there it was. I clicked on the first practitioner I saw, and I felt aligned right away. This veterinarian had been trained both in Western and Chinese medicine. She supported us in navigating care from both lenses. She has been an angel for us. Not only does she support our dog through a variety of healing modalities, but she has also lifted our spirits throughout the journey. It's been almost three years since the diagnosis and, with the exception of the occasional flare-up, our sweet animal is doing well!

Carrie

I have worn many hats throughout my life, including wife and mother to two amazing young men, and have had many successes, most recently achieving financial independence. I'm a very happy, capable, and grateful human who is an eternal optimist about myself and others.

But that wasn't always the case.

My childhood included parental alcoholism, divorce, death, and suicide, untreated mental illness, a stepmother who did not want me, and instability resulting in more than twenty moves and school changes with lack of any consistent shelter. By the time I was twenty-four, I found myself completely alone.

As one might imagine, the net-net of these events and traumas produced severe negative imprints of abandonment, FUD (fear, uncertainty, and doubt), and the inability to trust. I had no concept of self-care—only self-sabotage and people pleasing. I never learned to set boundaries. My daily fear of loss was so great that I thought something terrible would happen to my boys every time they left the house. I was lost, lacked meaning and purpose, and could not understand why I had even survived my childhood traumas.

Until the Universe stepped in and I met Monica and started working with my Team. With practice, I can now see, feel, and sense my Team's messages as well as my own intuition. Asking for and receiving validating signs from my Team has helped me to trust the guidance and take action, whereas before I would have ignored any perceived messages or intuitive suggestions.

Because of the Other Side, I no longer feel abandoned or alone. I am 100 percent confident that my Team and deceased relatives are fully engaged and focused on helping me, improving my future, and providing safety and security.

For example, red cardinals have appeared to me in random places ever since I was a kid, usually when I was going through a difficult period. It wasn't until just recently that I put it all together and fully understood that my Team has been sending me cardinals whenever they sensed I needed support.

Engaging with my Team has been nothing short of transformative to my health and wellbeing, my relationships, my decisions, my work/life balance, and most importantly, my self-care. The guidance I've received has given me a better understanding of who I actually am and why I am here. There is still lots of work to be done on this journey, but I know that I'm right where I'm supposed to be.

Last winter, I was experiencing pure burnout professionally. Personally, I was not in good health, overweight, and felt terrible. I knew I needed to trust the messages from my Team and that they would be there for me no matter what, and so I quit my job. I gave a two-month notice and said, "I'm out." I didn't have a plan but wasn't scared for a single moment.

Fast-forward one year, and I'm right where I want and need to be. I've gotten my nutrition in check, dropped thirty-five pounds, and my health markers have all improved. Not once has money or the cost of quitting hurt me. If anything, it has been the best financial investment I've ever made. I'm confident my Team guided me here.

Jennifer

Working with my Team has been one of the most magical gifts in my life.

As someone who struggles to trust myself and that I have the answer, I often turn to external sources like friends, partners, and family members during moments when I am faced with big decisions—especially around my career and life transitions.

Working with my Team has allowed me to anchor into my inner wisdom and connect with the part of me that knows that all the answers are within me. They are like an extension of me, and whenever I ask for their support, my Team shows up in the most wonderful ways.

When I first started working with the Other Side, I struggled to decipher and trust the signs. My Team responded by sending me confirmation through my body. I know a sign is real when I get a tingling sensation that starts at the crown of my head and moves down my throat and into my heart.

Over the years, through deep meditation and connecting with the Other Side, I've opened up to my own gifts and been able to identify my Team. I can physically feel their energy when they are present and can hear their wisdom for myself and others.

Most recently, my Team helped me manifest a new home in seven days. After thirteen years of living in the same home, I woke up one day and realized I was done living in a high-rise at the corner of a busy intersection in Toronto. But I had no idea where I was going to live, and finding a new place is never easy.

I knew this was an opportunity to ask my Team for help.

Right before I called our real estate agent, I said out loud to them, "Please help me find a beautiful place to live and show me signs that I'm heading in the right direction."

I closed my eyes and heard one of my guides speak clearly to me: "Call your brother's real estate agent—she has the place."

I picked up the phone and called her.

From the listings she sent over, there were two spots that caught my eye. One of them had my middle name in the street name. I felt the confirmation in my body that my Team had sent me a sign, so I asked to see that listing first.

As soon as we walked into the space, I heard my Team whisper, "Welcome home." The space was everything I envisioned in my meditation earlier in the day: quiet, lots of light, friendly owners, and it was down the street from a beautiful park (and farmer's market)!

As I left and walked out onto the street, I asked for one final sign that this was my home. I looked down and there at my feet was a white feather in the snow, one of the signs I use to know my Team is present.

Natalie

During a session with Monica, I really wanted to know what my deeper purpose was, but my Team wasn't ready to share. Or maybe I wasn't ready to receive it yet. Monica asked the Other Side multiple times, and all she could say was, "There are lots of veins." I had no idea what that meant at the time.

For the past decade, life had felt like I was climbing the same mountain over and over again, not feeling like I was making meaningful progress. I was worn out. I had been carrying around a fuzzy vision to create an education system that would raise awareness of the impact of light on our health, but I hadn't sorted out any details and didn't know what the "light" was yet.

The direction of my mission started to click on a nature walk when an idea came to me around the concept of supporting others on their mindfulness and intention-setting journeys. From my years of intentionality work and morning meditations, my Team further clarified that my role was to do so through education and inspiration.

Today I create wearable reminders in the form of temporary tattoos to help people stay present to what matters most. There are now thousands of people around the world applying my little Mindful Marks to their pressure points—and veins! I don't think Monica or I could've ever imagined that's what my Team meant. They are always pointing us in the right direction.

Malka

After Monica introduced me to my Team and how they were supporting me on my journey, I started acknowledging and speaking to them. The more I connected with my Team, the stronger my intuition became and the more aware I was of their messages coming in.

In 2019, I was guided to close my jewelry business of twenty years and was supported in every way to pursue my purpose. The Other Side often delivers messages to me as thoughts. I heard them say, "There will be a man who will come and buy all the showcases and fixtures from the shop. Give him a good deal."

And that's exactly how it happened. Someone on our street was opening a new store and offered to buy all our furniture.

Next, my Team was nudging me to transform my game room to my office and sacred space for me to expand and do my work. I followed and trusted the message, and now it gives me so much peace to create there.

These experiences have led me to be in partnership with my Team and trust the signs. I always ask for my Team's assistance in anything I do in my business, or ask for the next step in my mission. The Team always sends me messages about who is going to be my next teacher and which courses to take for my growth. I'm excited to see what is next for me.

Alka

I was going through a dark time in my life and was feeling lost. I had gone through a divorce a few years prior. Wanting love again, I began to wonder if and when it would appear. Not long after, I was invited to a function but was unsure about attending. Several times, I got a gut feeling that I needed to go. I knew the feeling was from my Team. I'm glad I listened because that's where I met my partner. It has been a couple of years now, and he has brought me so much joy and healed me in so many different ways.

I have also received messages from the Other Side about my purpose and how I can serve humanity. I was looking for courses to take when all of the sudden, my sister told me about a workshop she was going to take. I looked it up and felt very aligned with it. I asked my Team to confirm, and I got a feeling in my gut to go for it. I am so happy I listened. After the first workshop, I signed up for two more. These workshops have helped me release what no longer serves me, reclaim my power, and feel confident in my own skin.

I received several messages from the Other Side that told me I was ready to start my mission. Some of the messages came from people who confirmed that I was on the right path. Some came in the form of the right teachers and coaches appearing to support me on my journey. They all gave me confidence in myself and my gifts. I am now living my purpose.

I talk to my Team all the time. When I have a question or am not sure what to do about a situation, I ask for the same sign three times. It is amazing how fast it appears. I always get my answer. They are always there with me; I just have to ask for guidance with love.

Vik: Part One

I was in an accident at twenty-two years old that left me a paraplegic. The accident was the catalyst to my spiritual awakening, as it has led me down a conscious path to understand that I am a cocreator of my reality and could create empowerment from my situation.

During a reading with Monica, the Other Side shared with her that my healing journey was going to begin by going to meditation retreats and that I needed to get craniosacral work. I already had a massage therapist who had been helping me with my injuries. At our next session, she mentioned that she was studying craniosacral! I knew she had been sent by the Other Side as a healer for my journey and immediately began receiving craniosacral from her.

I was also led to attend a number of Dr. Joe Dispenza meditation retreats over the next the two years. These meditation retreats fell into my lap. They were definitely sent by the Other Side.

In 2019, I was working as a high school science teacher. I was still deep into meditation and spiritual work but no longer felt aligned with this career. I now know that that feeling was a directional gift from the Other Side. I kept receiving flashes of insight that it was time to move into this next position. I trusted the Other Side and allowed them to guide me toward this next phase of my life and mission as a spiritual teacher, speaker, and writer.

I had a strong feeling that it was time for me to move and reset my life for this new venture. The strong feeling kept getting clearer and clearer, so I decided to take the leap and move back home in the summer of 2019, and in August, I encountered a website developer whose experience aligned with my endeavors. I knew that there are no coincidences and that I was being sent this person to further me along. I was then set up with an appointment for headshots. At the photoshoot, the photographer was so interested in what I was doing that she said she was interested in being a client, as were her boyfriend and assistant. And that's how my business started.

From listening to nudges from the Other Side to taking the leaps and being in flow with their directional guidance, I also went on to become a published author. My first book was released in June of 2021.

Vik: Part Two

In October of 2020, I had a strong urge to visit Sedona. I knew Sedona had high spiritual energy, and I had just had an incredible experience in Mount Shasta, California that August, meeting spiritual people with many gifts who had become good friends. I was intrigued when the inspiration to travel to Sedona struck, but I decided to feel it out a little more and not make a preemptive decision.

A month later, I was talking to a friend who's psychically gifted. During our conversation, she said, "Are you thinking about going to Sedona? Because I'm getting if you're thinking about going that you should go." I was startled by her message because I hadn't mentioned anything to her about Sedona.

After this conversation, I told my Team, "Okay Team, if you want me to go to Sedona, I need you to give me one more sign."

A week later, a different friend who also knew nothing about the trip called me and said, "Yo man, I gotta tell you, I just came back from Sedona. You would love Sedona!"

I couldn't believe it. The message was clear, so a month later, I went to Sedona for four days. I was blown away by the beauty of the land, the energy, and the rich spiritual community there.

I returned home but couldn't get Sedona out of my mind. A friend who lived there had a townhouse, and the bottom floor studio apartment was available. Being a wheelchair user, I needed something suitable to my needs, and this space was perfect. Three weeks later, I moved to Sedona.

Three months later, I found a completely wheelchair accessible two-bedroom house to rent. This place was literally made for a wheelchair, equipped with ramps, handlebars...the whole thing. I signed the lease and stayed in Sedona for an additional six months. I spent most of the year in this high-vibration city that helped me heal many emotions and develop my energetic and intuitive gifts in the process. It was a lesson in trusting my Team's messages and following through, knowing that they have a greater plan that's always in my highest good.

CHAPTER 15

Chase You

We spend our lives chasing. The job, the money, the relationship, the body, the house, the car, even the kids—anything that we think will make us happy.

We chase likes and comments from strangers. We chase highlight reels instead of real life. We chase everything but ourselves.

We listen to friends, family, coworkers. We look to the Jones', celebrities, and the media to tell us who we should emulate and what we should strive for, only the target keeps moving and the chase never ends.

You is worth chasing. *You* is who you came here to be, before life happened and shit happened and someone or many someones told you you weren't enough.

We're so busy chasing things, but true, long-lasting happiness lies in being of service and making a difference in a way that's aligned with your soul's purpose.

No matter who you are or where you come from, the color of your skin or the place you worship, who you love, the shape of your body or the size of your bank account, you can work with the Other Side to have a life of joy. It's not magic, but it is magical.

Our challenge to you is to get clear on your definition of success and what makes YOU happy. Get clear on the gifts only you have and the mission only you can fulfill. Then get busy chasing you so that you can support the community you came here to serve and the legacy you signed up to leave. The Other Side is ready when you are.

EPILOGUE

Real Talk: Commonly Asked Questions About Working with the Other Side

Over the years of working with Monica, I have peppered her with questions about the Other Side—even when I already know the answer. There's nothing more reassuring than hearing it from the expert, who has them on speed-dial. I don't know where she gets the patience for endless texts and voice memos, some more whiny and desperate than is becoming of a grown woman, but I'd be lost without her reassuring responses. Below is a compilation of our typical exchanges, which also reflect the most frequently asked questions she gets from clients. I hope it's the next best thing to a direct line to Monica.

—*Elizabeth*

Monica. What do you mean you can see your Team? Like, are they standing in the room right now?

Our teams are always with us. As I have always said, they are with us from the moment we are born to the moment we go back. They never leave our side. This is a great question because there are different ways that I can see them. When I had the near-death experience and when I tune in for clients, I can physically see them. What I mean by this is that I see them just like I would see you standing in front of me. They appear to be in physical form. There are other times that I see what I call orbs or specks of light. This typically happens when I am not tuning in for a client. I will see a tiny speck of light quickly flashing around me. They are either white or purple. I find that when I am deep in thought or worried about something, the tiny lights will appear to let me know they are with me.

Now if I am not tuned in, and let's say I am standing talking to you, I will feel your Team appear because they might have something to say. The feeling is like when someone is walking behind you and you don't know it, but you feel it. If I want to see them, then I have to focus my awareness on them in order to see them. My close family and friends who have experienced this with me say that I will look to their side as they are talking to me and I zone out as if I am not listening to them—LOL. It's very true because I find that I start focusing on them to see them. When I focus on them, I will get a clear, physical picture in my mind of what they look like. Most of the time I won't do this because I can hear them clearly and I don't have to see them to receive the messages. That way, I can still continue having a conversation while receiving the messages.

Is my Team around me too? Why can't I see them?

They are around you. Every soul can hear, see, feel, and/or know the Other Side. It takes practice...a lot of practice. Once I agreed to do this mission, I rigorously studied to enhance my skills. I took every class imaginable, read a ton of books, researched the greats before me, and studied with some amazing spiritual teachers. It's like any new skill. If you want it, you will work for it. If I was going to do this work, I wanted to make sure I was great at it. You and everyone else also have these skills. I would highly recommend that everyone familiarize themselves with the spiritual gifts they were given so they can cocreate their lives with the Other Side. There is a ton of information available to us all from the souls that have gone through this before us.

I'm not religious, I'm a recovering Catholic. The idea of angels makes me uncomfortable. Discuss.

I grew up in a strong Catholic household. In fact, my mother dedicated all her time to her Catholic church until her transition back over. Angels are written and spoken about in all faiths. Thankfully, most of my clients are very open to this arena. But for those who are seeking and trying to figure it all out, I like to tell them that their higher being is like the CEO and the angels are like the VPs. They all love and care about us equally, but we get to have a beautiful team of them designated to each one of us!

Do they have wings? Wait—maybe don't answer that.

LOL. I have seen wings. Some have physical forms and look like we do, some look like the typical angel form we are used to seeing in pictures with wings, and some look like beings of glowing light.

I keep asking for a sign about fill-in-the-blank and they haven't sent me one.

There are different reasons for not receiving a sign. First, make sure you keep the sign you are requesting super simple. When you're new to this practice, I always suggest starting with a simple request like to see a coin, a butterfly, or a feather. Those are easy for them to make appear.

The second thing I would suggest is to be sure you pay attention. Remember, signs can come in the physical form like an object, or they can come in the form of a picture, an email, a billboard, or even someone mentioning the item. It could even be a song that is playing on the radio that has "feather" in the title.

To be safe, I always ask for the same sign three times within three days. That way, I am hit over the head with the sign—LOL.

How do I know these signs aren't just a coincidence but actually from my Team?

I am here to tell you there is no such thing as a coincidence. They are always events, opportunities, guidance, and/or signs from the Other Side!

I followed the signs and they were WRONG!

Signs are never wrong. Where we think they are wrong is when we have expectations of an outcome. Signs are like breadcrumbs. You have to follow them with faith and trust that they are leading you to something or someone for your highest good. Where we get in trouble is when we think we know where a breadcrumb was "supposed" to take us and it didn't happen the way we thought it "should" happen.

There might be times when we misinterpret a sign. That is okay. The Other Side will always course-correct us. Typically, a pivot is all it takes us to get back into alignment.

Do you ever have doubts about the Other Side?

No, I do not. Now with that said, at the beginning when I was first learning to work with the Other Side, I would question A LOT! However, each time, they would show me they were always right. It was more about me learning to have faith and trust in them.

What about when we do lose faith? I have personally had moments when I feel abandoned by my Team and it's the worst.

This can definitely happen. We tend to get impatient, or we want the assistance to look a certain way or be delivered in the way we want it delivered. Remember, they are the teachers and we are the students. They deliver the lesson plan and opportunities to us in their own way. It's okay to feel angry, confused, or frustrated. Feel and name the emotion. Cry it out if you have to, but release the emotion after you have processed it. Then regroup and send an SOS to your Team. They will always deliver. Here's a little hint: typically, when you lose faith, the answer is around the corner.

Have you ever ignored the signs? What happened?

I have ignored a sign or two—LOL. During my college years, I was working for a place that I loved. It was a healthcare clinic that served the indigent. I loved the work, my boss, and the staff because their hearts were in work. In fact, that is the very first place that I had ever heard the word "mission," which you know now plays an important role in my life. I worked my way up the ranks while finishing school. When it was time for me to graduate, everyone kept asking me, "What are you going to do now? Where are you going to apply? Are you ready to make the big bucks?"

The societal and family pressures were so real. Everyone had the same definition of success and were pressuring me with it. I decided to go and talk to my two bosses at the time, and they assured me that if I was patient, I would move up in the organization. I was so happy to hear this because I truly loved and valued the outreach this organization was doing for the community. I loved going to work and being part of a beautiful team that was serving a deserving community.

As you can imagine, I kept being pressured about getting a "real" job and making "real" money. I started doubting myself. My knowing. I started applying for other "real" jobs, and I wasn't being called for interviews. This was a first for me. I was used to getting the interview and receiving job offers. I was shocked at the lack of opportunities that were coming my way. In the meantime, my bosses would periodically come in and tell me to keep waiting. I kept telling the Universe that I wanted a "real" job. Finally, a friend of a friend put my name in the hat to interview at a big tech company that everyone was dying to work for. Strangely, the position was in my degreed field, paid way more than I was making, and seemed like an exciting opportunity. I interviewed and received a job offer.

I went to work at the new tech company and immediately knew I had made a mistake. I hated every minute of it. This was to no fault of the company; I was just not with my people. I was miserable. I kept looking for an opening back at my previous organization. but there was nothing. I was so unhappy and was kicking myself because I had ignored messages to be patient and wait. I chose to allow societal and familial definitions of success to pressure me into leaving something I truly loved. Thankfully, I had been praying hard to get my old job back. I had almost given up hope and accepted that I would have to pay the price for my mistake for a long time when I received my pivot! After six months on the job, my prior bosses called to say that a position had been created and they wanted me back! I've never jumped so fast in my life without thinking about it. My course-correct had arrived.

Will my Team give up or stop helping me if I don't follow the signs?

Our Team will never give up, stop helping us, or leave us. They are with us from the minute we get here until the moment we go back. I can't say this enough. The only time they don't assist us is when we don't grant them permission. They can't interfere so we have to grant them permission. (See Chapter 5!)

It's in your timeline that was predestined before you arrived. Sadly, it's us who get in the way when we try to control everything and don't allow the Other Side to bring it to us. We take action before allowing and then moving into action. We allow societal and familial pressures to define our choices and determine our actions. We feel wrong if we don't follow what we're "supposed" to do. We allow others to dictate what we should look like, what our partnerships should look like, what success looks like, what money should be used for, and timelines for us. Becoming very clear about what you want is the silver bullet you need to bring in your desires. A bit of wisdom for you is to make sure you authentically know yourself. Knowing your authentic self is the catalyst for bringing everything in.

But I followed all of the steps! I know who I am! Why don't they bring it to meeeeee?

Trust and faith. We want it when we want it. We don't realize that the Other Side has to make sure you are ready for it. If we learn to have patience, as the old saying goes, "Good things come to those who wait." PATIENCE is huge when working with the Other Side. I know this might be hard for some people to hear, but patience is truly is a virtue. Take it from this recovering Type A personality: patience is so worth it. I would recommend choosing to have fun while you're being patient. It will keep your vibrational energy in a joyous state.

Why is the Other Side punishing me?

The Other Side will absolutely NEVER punish anyone. They only communicate through love. Sadly, we don't realize that we are our own jail keepers, our worst critics, and we tend to get in our own way. The Other Side works through love. I have never heard them say a single unkind word. Their vibrational level is too high to do anything energetically low. Punishing is a low vibrational frequency. The Other Side loves us and wants to help us in any way possible. They don't judge, think less of, or punish us in any way. On the contrary, they love us and will course-correct us when needed. They see and work with nothing but love.

I'm still angry with my Team for not giving me what I want—is that allowed?

Well, I have been known to throw a fit or two. There are times when I am not understanding, lose my patience, and get frustrated. I tend to throw epic tantrums on these occasions. I personally think it's okay to lose your sh*t. It allows all the pent-up energy to leave your body and soul. Doing so almost always provides the solutions to what is ailing you. The Other Side is very loving and understanding. And that's why I always apologize after I get angry.

Is this a joke? I can't possibly quit my job/leave my partner/move across the country!

Oh, yes you can...when you are ready. There are some people who are blessed with the gift of adventure. Those people jump without thinking. I applaud them, but I am not one of them. What has helped me with this process is tuning into my authentic self. I ask myself, "Will this bring me happiness? Will this bring me closer to my mission?" Knowing that your Team will always course-correct you along the way if needed definitely helps out!

If this is my mission, why is it so hard?

When you are in alignment with your mission, most things go smoothly. However, we are in "earth school," as Oprah calls it. We are always learning. Some things are harder than others. If we go in knowing that some of our lessons might be harder than others, we are more prepared. If something feels hard, then I would recommend you dive in deep to the experience and see what it is teaching you. The answer always appears to teach you when you are ready.

But I thought my life would be perfect if I followed the signs!

First of all, there is no such thing as perfection. That is something the Other Side stresses. We are here to love, to learn, and to advance. With this comes difficulties and wins. Without one, we can't have the other. When I am struggling with something, I immediately move into self-care mode. A little TLC for yourself goes a long way. It plugs you back into peace and clarity so you can pick yourself back up and keep moving forward. The key is awareness—awareness in knowing that you are struggling, awareness in knowing how to soothe yourself, and awareness that everything is going to be okay.

I don't have the energy for the people or activities that I used to. What is happening to me?

Believe it or not, this is a good sign. We live at vibrational levels. Imagine yourself in a kiddy pool. You can hang in the kiddy pool, you have things in common with the people in the kiddy pool, and your awareness resides in that kiddy pool. One day, you decide that you've had enough of the kiddy pool and you decide to take swim lessons. Now you are in the big pool with people who can swim in the kiddy pool. You have now "joined" a different vibrational level. Your needs and wants are growing, and you are now surrounded by those with the same needs and wants.

You will become tired during your swimming lessons, a.k.a. your growth. You will now have more in common with the bigger-pool friends, so your activities will change as well. The best way to help yourself is by honoring your feelings and wants. Honor your body if it's tired, wants to nap or sleep, if it wants to eat more than usual, or watch Netflix all day! And if you don't want to hang out in the kiddy pool anymore, you don't have to. Don't judge yourself or try to push through it. Honor your body and self!

All of this spiritual work is too much. Can I take a break?

I have definitely taken breaks! I remember in the beginning I would tell my husband that I was quitting! My best friend and I sometimes call each other threatening to tap out (insert eye roll emoji). Breaks are always good. Take as long as you would like! The Other Side wants us to nurture and nourish ourselves, so if that's what you need, do it!

About the Authors

Eliesa Johnson

Elizabeth Kendig

The founder of Healerswanted.com, host of *Healers* podcast, and the Head of Content at WellSet, Elizabeth Kendig has dedicated her career to taking the weird out of the woo and making spiritual and holistic practices more accessible. Previously, she served as a magazine editor, editorial director for Fortune 500 companies, and an accidental influencer with an award-winning beauty blog, coveted skincare line, and more than five million Pinterest followers. She and her work have appeared in *Allure*, justBOBBI, *Glamour*, *InStyle*, *Martha Stewart Living*, *People*, *Rue Magazine*, the *Today* show, and more. She lives in the Bay Area.

Bill Lawson

Monica Lawson

Monica Lawson is a first-generation Latina from healer lineage. As a sought-after Spiritual Advisor, she uses her gifts to help clients around the world discover their purpose, connect with the Other Side, and cocreate a life of joy. She gives readings to people from all walks of life, including celebrated actors, TV and movie producers and directors, Grammy award-winning singers and songwriters, Silicon Valley executives, and fellow spiritual teachers. Although her clients range in age from eleven to eighty, they're all looking for the same thing: to find their mission. She lives in Austin, TX.

Advance Praise for
CHASE *YOU*

"Elizabeth is the soul sister and friend everyone needs: spiritual without being too woo, wise without taking herself too seriously, and hilarious enough to keep up with me. To have her candid voice and storytelling in book form makes this essential reading for anyone seeking self-actualization. So everyone."

—**Paula Froelich**, *New York Times* bestselling author and on-air correspondent for *NewsNation*

"Mental health is going to be mission-critical in a post-pandemic world. We need a broad set of accessible holistic tools, including the ones in this book, to support people across all backgrounds on their path to well-being."

—**Christina Mack**, PhD, MSPH, FISPE, Epidemiologist

"The knowledge and energy that Monica brings from the other side is so needed in our world right now. She does a beautiful job in teaching us to connect with our spiritual team to guide and help us in our lives, which I have also experienced personally. Monica's spiritual gift is to elevate the vibration of our world, which makes her the perfect person to write this book and continue to raise the consciousness of humanity."

—**Alka Vaswani**, Infinite Love Center Co-Founder, McAllen, TX